MW00627058

CRUSH THE PINK SLIP
Get Back to Work in 60 Days

Published by Push Career Management, LLC
Laveen, AZ 85339
www.royalresumeaz.com

ISBN 978-0-9967539-0-6 (paperback)
ISBN 978-0-9967539-1-3 (electronic)

Cover by Riddick Agency, Phoenix, AZ
Editing by LaToya Rosario, Dallas, TX

This book contains stories in which the author has changed people's names and some details of their situations in order to protect their privacy.

Printed in the United States of America

This book is available at quantity discounts for bulk purchases. For information, send an email to info@pushcareermanagement.com.

Dedication

I dedicate this work to you brave job seekers who are bold enough to subscribe to a real plan and execute it. You who refuse to settle for just anything, but you who strive toward that specific thing that brings you satisfaction and allows you to make meaningful contributions to this world!

Acknowledgements

With my whole heart, I acknowledge my heavenly Father and my earthly father, Al Moye. Thanks for giving me the best life imaginable.

To my amazing husband, Patrick, and the best children I could have ever asked for, Miles and Nacol: Thank you for being my biggest cheerleaders as I crossed the finish line and completed this book. To my mother, Linda D., I thank you for always encouraging me even when no one else did.

To my aunties: Brenda, thank you for being the best volunteer employee in the history of the world, and to Deanna, thank you for sharing all of your management stories which are represented throughout this book, and I pray that you and I continue to help people navigate their careers.

To Pastor Ricky Wilson, you may never fully know how much you encouraged me with a single word — PUSH!

To the magnificent Mag 6: You ladies keep raising the bar, and it causes me to fight harder than I knew I could. Thank you!

To my assistant, La'Vista Jones: Thanks for keeping "the enforcer," accountable to someone. Your business management has been excellent! To the meticulous LaToya Rosario: You have been such a tremendous blessing in my life. Thank you for your wonderful gift of editing!

Finally, I acknowledge The National Resume Writers' Association, and the Resume Writer's Council of Arizona. You've all poured into me and helped me to become a more confident career manager. Thank you for your priceless gift.

CONTENTS

Crush the Pink Slip

Introduction / My Layoff Story

"Brenda, will you come with me for a moment?" That's what my boss said as he gave me the dreaded tap on the shoulder. I had just finished lunch on a seemingly regular Wednesday afternoon. The tap on the shoulder came as I dialed into one of the standing conference calls regarding one of the nine concurrent projects I was managing (that one was only expected to save the company a few million dollars). In my own mental bubble I believed that I was untouchable. I was valuable. I brought order to the chaos that my projects had formerly seen, and we were making tangible progress toward realizing the projected cost savings. Soon, and very soon, I would discover it wasn't enough. I followed my boss into the abyss of that private conference room, and it happened. "Brenda, we have to let you go. Please know that it has nothing to do with your abilities, contributions, or work ethic, rather we have to trim a percentage of our team and you were the last person hired." So essentially, because I came late to the party, I was the first to be ejected. The old business adage of Last In First Out, or LIFO, proved true. Although they were telling me that it wasn't me, I couldn't help but to call my own confidence into question.

We returned to my cubicle. I packed my boxes as my boss hovered nearby, likely to make sure I didn't walk out with any proprietary information. I tried my best to hold back the tears until I could escape to my vehicle of solitude. I almost made a clean break when I bumped into a friend on my way out with box of shame in hand, and I broke down. I told her I couldn't talk then but I would call her later. I made it to the car, "Whew!" I called my husband, my sister, and my mother, explaining the confidence-striking story over and over again each time adding details I had previously forgotten. Finally, I got home to my quiet house. Thank God the kids were still in daycare, and I was able to cry all by myself. I felt anger and sadness—those I recognized. But this blindsiding, devastating blow pulverized my confidence! I had been hurled into a world with which I was unfamiliar. I didn't know how to live in this place. I told you, it was a Wednesday, but it wasn't until Monday that I decided to get up off the couch and get busy.

My company offered outplacement services with a well-known local firm so I made an appointment to come in and get the overview of how they could help me re-enter the rat race. I went and to my surprise, I saw so many others from my former team, miserably push themselves into that outplacement office. I saw amazing talent represented there and suddenly, I realized that perhaps it wasn't me because after all, if they let these superstars leave, then it must just be that the company is really suffering. That satisfied me for the moment, but those racing thoughts of insufficiency would creep up again and again. Clearly, I wasn't good enough for them to keep me! Perhaps I had fooled everyone for my nine years as an engineer and project manager in corporate America and my fraudulent ways finally caught up with me. Who knows? I fed myself, so many lies I vaguely remember half of them. All I knew was discouragement.

I pretended to look for a job for about another month. All the while I was really just lying on the couch all day, eating, watching TV, and drowning in my own sea of self-pity. Occasionally, I would show a spark of interest in the outside world and check in with the outplacement firm, but to no avail. To me, that was the most useless investment my company could have made. They offered surface level resume feedback, gave us a list of recruiters, offered access to yet another job board, and opened their office to us if we needed to make copies or phone calls. Copies? Phone calls? I could do that stuff at home. Why would I use my gas to go to their office when I had the silence of my home to accommodate my outreach needs? What I really need was encouragement, accountability, and a real plan of attack.

Oh pity! I didn't get what I needed from the outplacement firm. Thank God, I was ultimately able to pull myself off that couch and start brushing the dust of rejection off of my soul so I could be unburdened and get myself back into the workforce. But where do I start? What do I even want to do? I finally had the opportunity to ask myself what I wanted. You see I'd never really thought about that before and I realized that this layoff gave me a gift—the priceless gift of defining what I really wanted from my career. Finally, I had a dormant season where I was not completely consumed with my work so I could focus on my skills, interests, and passions. You see I did what most professionals do, I gave 100 percent to the job and had nothing left over for me! When you're constantly fighting fires at work, when exactly are you supposed to make time to plan your career? Well, the bottom line is that you have to make time! Time is not magical, and it does not mysteriously appear, we have to prioritize the things that must happen in our days, weeks, months, or years.

So what happened? I'll tell you what happened. I drew my line in the sand. I got serious, and I finally told someone else about my challenges over those past few months. And with external eyes paying attention, a newfound motivation was ignited in me. I decided that I didn't have to have all the answers, but a solid direction to get started would help. For me, since I had found myself thriving as a project manager, of course I would pursue project management opportunities. But the specific applications I previously supported, did not inspire me. So I said to myself, "Self, what really matters to me?" I actually answered myself. "Education, healthcare, and manufacturing products that would make a real difference in the world." I realized that it was really hard for me to care about a semiconductor application that would allow your cellphones to toggle between portrait and landscape displays with a simple rotation. Since I had this opportunity for a new beginning, this time I would do it right. I would open my eyes to what would make me feel like I was having an impact on the world. So you see, what seemed like a nightmare actually turned out to be a blessing. It was the wake-up call I needed.

I circulated a few resumes, asked for a few referrals, nothing too consistent though. I did just enough to look like a "serious" job seeker. Then my phone rang! Finally! A recruiter found my resume and wanted me to come in for a meeting. It went fabulously. We had instant chemistry, and she had the perfect manufacturing opportunity for me to explore. They produced oral cancer screening kits and in my mind, this was important. I interviewed. Everything went perfectly, perhaps a little too perfectly. The feedback was, we really like Brenda but she seems a little too good. We fear that when the economy recovers, she'll be off to greener pastures. They considered me a flight risk. And with another candidate willing to accept $15k less than I, they extended their offer to my competitor. About one month later, I received another, albeit unexpected phone call for an education sales opportunity. After being in this stopgap job for a little over a year, I realized that I was still not doing meaningful work (for me). I had this heart to help people who wanted to help themselves but didn't have the knowledge or resources to get there, and following a 3-day fasting and prayer journey with God, my true calling had been revealed to me. A few months later, I quit my job and started running my business full time.

I didn't share that with you so you could quit your job and launch a business (unless that is your calling as well). I shared it so you could have a real life example of a real life career transitioner. It's not always a crystal clear road that you'll travel on. You won't always have all the answers. You may accept some less-than-perfect opportunities along the way, but if you have three things: (1) a goal, (2) a game plan, and (3) dangerous expectations, then true career satisfaction will be yours for the taking.

It's crazy but it's real: You don't have to dread Sunday nights and hate Monday mornings. There is such a thing as a career that brings you satisfaction and consistent joy. Often times the challenge is "I know what I want to do, what would bring me happiness, but I have no idea how to get it." That is why this book was written. It is an easily digestible guide for the professional who is facing an unexpected job search. It will show you success stories, examples, ask you questions, challenge you, and show you how to move toward and thrive within your ideal career. The process is threefold with a bonus:

Identify what your ideal career is. You will be able to clearly describe what it looks like, how much you'll get paid, and how your next role will help you claim your big picture vision.

Learn how to execute your well-thought-out plan. This book will help you with scripts, timelines, interview strategies, and even negotiating your salary/compensation packages.

Keep your mind steady and focused to remain encouraged throughout your journey. Along the way, just like it did with me discouragement and depression tried to settle in and take up residence in my mind. You'll need tools to combat those negatives.

Bonus: Start your new role on the right foot and set the stage for future promotions and growth as you move throughout your career. You will learn what do in the first 90 days to ensure your future success. It's certainly not enough to just get a job, owning your career is a sure sign of a confident career transitioner.

This systematic approach is designed like shampoo; you can wash, rinse, repeat! You can reproduce your results time and time again as you navigate throughout your career, and this book will be your ferocious weapon that you can wield as needed.

How to Further Maximize the Content of this Book

Now remember, I am a coach, one who helps my clients to see their own awesomeness! So there will be a lot of things that challenge you to change your perspective. But I am also a practical woman, and I refuse for this book to be another hurdle on your career transition hurdle. With this in mind, this book is organized into four sections: Goals, Game Plan, Dangerous Expectations, and The First 90 Days. I suggest you read them in order, but within each section there will be days where the information won't resonate with you. It's OK; just skip that days' entry and move on to something more relevant. Also, I chose this format because a lot of change can happen in 60 days, but we tend to overwhelm ourselves with big books, big actions, and big goals. So I've broken it down for you so you can digest this great information one day at a time.

Change Is Really Hard But

Throughout my nine-year career within corporate America, I hated going to work. I often felt like a square peg in a round hole. I didn't fit in with my teams. They cared way too much about the work, and I only wanted to socialize and run the meetings. I wanted my work to stop at 5pm, but it kept going. Conference calls with China, Korea, Malaysia. Then, I was up early the next day for a 7am shouting match with the senior leaders to discuss why their unrealistic expectations wouldn't be met. My teams were constantly overloaded and as a result, they missed deadlines for my programs. Their priorities were constantly shifting, and I'm not sure we ever hit an actual planned milestone. I knew I needed a change, but I didn't have time to think about it amidst all the fires I was paid to extinguish. Yet, I was laid off. Finally, free to dream and think about what I wanted, what mattered to me. Lo and behold, it wasn't manufacturing at all. It was education. Counseling and encouraging professionals to pursue the career paths they desired. I had found my calling. Since then,

I dropped the veil of "security" and launched my business full-time to guide other career changers into their ideal careers. That was my path, which may have never been discovered if not for my layoff. Truly, I am happier than I've ever been.

Losses Lead to Gains: For years, I had noticed my belly flab getting larger and larger. It really bothered me and eventually none of my clothes would fit. You would think I'd do something about it, and I did—I bought bigger clothes. Then, I watched it continue to grow and live there on the inside of me. I knew I could do something about it, but I felt powerless to take action. On some level, I knew what I needed to do, but it seemed so big that I did nothing. Then my coach, told me to just put in 15 minutes a day—have a green smoothie, walk my kids to school, and meditate. That was it! Because I had a realistic, practical plan and I knew she was watching, I put my plan into motion and I've seen results and a 15-pound weight loss as of July 2015. Bottomline: Taking on big tasks one day at a time and having a guide with a side of accountability is the easiest path to start seeing a real difference in your situation. So let's go through this together!

PART I – GOALS

Do the opposite of what most people do when they launch a career transition.

If you think following the strategies in this book is uncomfortable, try living on unemployment for a year (or more)! There are no more barriers to your rapid return to the workforce.

READY, FIRE, AIM!
THE IMPORTANCE OF AIM
DAY ①

When most people launch a job search, they do it as if they are trying to build a complex machine without the assembly instructions. Successfully landing in a new career takes skill, knowledge, connections, referrals, and resources, but if you don't know what type of career or job you wish to have then to whom will you call upon for referrals? Which connections should you leverage? That's right, it's impossible to execute a plan when you don't know where you're going.

Have you ever had the itch to get out of the house and go somewhere? The problem with this is that you don't know what you should wear, if you'll need directions, or how long to schedule the babysitter. You know you want to get out, but without a plan or target, you'll end up with chaos on your hands. You might find yourself at a nightclub dressed for the gym, or at a fancy restaurant without enough cash on hand to cover the bill.

In his timeless classic, Think and Grow Rich, Napoleon Hill declared, "There is one quality which one must possess to win, and that is definiteness of purpose, the knowledge of what one wants and a burning desire to possess it."[1]

I often hear job seekers say things like, "I'll do anything; I just need a job." OK, so the gas station has a few openings, are you interested? "Well, no," is said in response. "I'm really looking for something in the IT field, perhaps in the area of network security."

Have you ever seen one of those suspense movies, and the mysterious agent gets in a cab and says, "Just drive"? The cab driver is always so confused. The driver wants something more specific; he needs a destination. Even if they are inclined to just start driving, there will be so many questions along the way: questions of uncertainty that could have been avoided with a simple exclamation of where you wanted to go.

The moral: It's difficult to be decisive, but it's necessary to avoid a lot of doubt creep and wasted time as you embark on this career transition.

Application Tip:

Vow to never again say, I just need a job! Always be more specific. I'm looking for _____ (your profession) opportunities in the field of_____

(Example: Engineering opportunities in the field of metrology, or IT positions in the area of network security).

KNOW YOUR WHY!
DAY ②

People, specifically employers, always want to know your "why," —your reason for why you are pursuing this specific opportunity—so it's great to know it for yourself. I remember once I was interviewing for a position as a packaging engineer, but I hadn't done it before and the interviewer had asked why I would apply for that role. I confidently explained that I had supported the packaging function during one of my previous roles, and I loved how much of an impact the material selection and confirmation of proper internal connections had on the overall functionality of a device. I explained how I had worked on wire diagrams and understood a little about material interaction but that I was hungry to know more and really contribute in this way. They must have appreciated my answer because I ended up getting the job and working as a packaging engineer for the next four years of my career.

You will be asked for your "why" so it's great to take a moment, pause, and consider why you're doing what you're doing. Here are some scenarios to get your mind churning:

New career direction: "I'm ready for something new."

Seeking a promotion: "I have operated in the role as a manager and leader and know it is my time for a promotion."

New self-discovery: "During the time I have been laid off, I have discovered my love of" or "I have found an excitement for_____."

Craving a new challenge: "While I have enjoyed the work I have been doing, I am interested in expanding my knowledge and experience by taking on different challenges and projects."

Returning to the workforce: "Although, I have been out of the traditional workforce for a period of time, I still desire to work in the _____ field."

Make sure your "why" is much bigger than the fact you were laid off. It must be deeper than that! It should be moving you toward some bigger vision that you can see clearly in your mind. The "why" question will constantly come up. Why did you leave your last job? Why this department? Why did you pursue a PhD? Why are you asking for this salary? Prepare your responses.

Application Tips:

Encourage yourself: You're going to go to work anyway, why not do what you want, and get paid what you deserve?

Exercise: Now that you have a clear career goal, what's your why? Write down your reasons for making this specific career move. Include enough detail so that if someone else were to read it, they could understand it.

Crush the Pink Slip

_____

_____

_____

_____

_____

_____

_____

_____

CAREER MAPPING
DAY ③

Just because you're unemployed at the moment doesn't mean you can't have a vision for the future of your career. If you can't see beyond today's rut, how will you truly know when a great opportunity is presenting itself?

Having a go-to career map or career plan can be one of the most valuable items you could ever possess. I'm not just talking about writing something on a post-it note and never looking at it again. I'm referring to a document that you can and will reference many times per year; if not daily or weekly, then at least monthly or quarterly. You will use this tool to remind yourself of your bigger goal.

A five-year career plan includes the following:

- My future position title

- Deadline

- Skills/Credentials I Need

- Other Info

Look at the example entries, which are part of one person's career plan, then use the empty spaces to create your own plan.

My Future Position Title	Deadline	Skills/Credentials I Need	Other Info
Ex. Part I - Promotion to Project Manager	2 years (by December 2016)	Obtain PMP, Request to lead a project team (gain experience)	Start networking with the PMO community. Startworking with the PMO community.
Ex. Part II - Director of Operations	3 years (by December 2019)	Finish MBA, Request finance project (to gain budgeting experience)	Take on at least one, high-visibility project

Throughout this planning process, talk to a mentor, review performance reviews to identify trends, and understand if opportunities exist where you are or if you'll need to relocate. What new languages do you need to learn (programming or speech)? What budget will you need to plan for to be successful? What conferences do you need to attend? What social networking platforms do you need to be active on? What committees or organizations could I partner with (volunteer) to gain additional exposure and experience? Also, consider industry preference, your desire to manage people, company size, and salary target.

Application Tips:

Year 1: Focus on skills, fill in gaps, and understand the pathway to your goal.

Year 2: Since I understand that I will need at least __ years of experience, I need to obtain _____ position by _____.

Years 3-4: Maximize your time in this role. Learn the nuances of leadership, overcome weaknesses, and look ahead to future job descriptions to ensure you're acquiring the needed skills, now.

Year 5: Arrive and map out the next five years. Repeat cycle.

IT'S OK TO HAVE STANDARDS
DAY ④

When my husband had lost his job of seven years, it was a devastating blow to his confidence. He was in the, I've-got-to-do-something-to-provide-for-my-family zone. We immediately updated his resume, talked about his interests, and his future career targets. Then, he started applying for jobs like a mad man and for the first few weeks the situation was looking quite positive. The phone was ringing off the hook, he had interviews galore, and he was sure that most of those would turn into offers.

They didn't.

Another month went by and it was more of the same. You could almost see his mental shift happening. He would begin lowering his standards. His salary expectations started to get lower and lower, his commute tolerance got longer and longer. This is so common. When recently unemployed people aren't seeing instant results, they can begin to panic. But it's OK to have standards! It's OK to know what you want to do, how much you want to make, what kind of hours you're willing to work, how long of a commute you're willing to have, how many days you need to work from home, and so on.

Think about the last time you were on a first date. You

24

probably had some sort of standards, or at least I hope you did. If your date showed no interest in their appearance, didn't look you in the eye, only talked about previous relationships, and was an overall slob, then it is highly likely that he or she didn't meet your high expectations. Similarly to your selection of career and job opportunities, more than 70 percent of your life will be given to your work, so you must have a set of standards by which you evaluate each opportunity.

Application Tip:

Please allow at least two to six months for your transition to be complete. This may be significantly shorter for internal postings but for external career/industry changes, temper your expectations and begin your process as early as possible to avoid frustration and desperation later.

STOP CROSSING BRIDGES WHEN YOU GET THERE

DAY ⑤

In his book, How Successful People Think, John Maxwell suggests that saying you'll cross that bridge when you get there, means that you have no vision of the bigger picture.[2] I can't tell you how many meetings I've been in during my corporate career where that was the response to a really important question. Then, what happened? Once we arrived, everyone would scramble to try and figure out our next move. There was no game plan, only good ideas that were potentially leading us nowhere—or worse yet, away from our goal.

Take Dee, a successful architect, who was perfectly content with her current situation, but knew she wanted more from her career eventually. With a new baby on the way, stability was priority No. 1. Staying put was an acceptable solution for now, but she proactively reached out to me to ensure that her resume was ready to go. As soon as the baby started to sleep through the night, Dee's career-change itch returned. She wanted more from her career. More income. More responsibility. More leadership influence.

She was emboldened to engage her director and state her demands. I want more money, more responsibility, and leadership influence. She was confident in her market attractiveness since she had posted her resume and received two calls within two hours. You see, before that, she had started to question her own abilities. She knew she wouldn't be out in the cold as she was highly sought after, so she went for it. Dee told me that her resume helped her to see her worth and to fight those feelings of self-doubt. She said, "You must be ready for what's next!"

So what happened in the end? Her boss asked her to stay, gave her a major raise, a major promotion, and her confidence is now unstoppable.

If Dee had crossed that bridge when she got there, the day would've likely never arrived.

Application Tips:

I'm guilty of it, too, but we often go through the motions of life and rarely take time to seek out direction or vision for the future. Pause, schedule time today, and meditate on what your future looks like. You should walk away from this time knowing the following:

1. Your ideal job title in 1-2 years

2. Your target salary

3. If your current career is where you'd like to stay for the foreseeable future

4. If your family is on board with any major career changes

5. If you are truly happy where you are or if you've just been tolerating your situation

"Self-awareness is impossible when you are on autopilot."

— ***Valorie Burton***

CAREER VS. JOB
DAY 6

Though the terms career and job are used interchangeably in everyday conversation, the words have noteworthy differences that can affect how you approach this process.

Let's start by defining each word. I'll go straight to the Merriam-Webster dictionary (my favorite) for this one.

> Career - A field for or pursuit of consecutive progressive achievement especially in public, professional, or business life. A profession for which one trains and which is undertaken as a permanent calling. A course. A series of jobs leading you toward a higher goal.

> Job - A piece of work. Something that has to be done. A specific duty, role, or function. To do odd or occasional pieces of work for hire.

To me, the difference is time. A job is meant to be a single part of your overall career. Your career spans the entire course of your working life while your job is a temporary application of your skillset that contributes to the whole of your career.

- You may have a career in IT, but your jobs may include network administrator, database manager, and server architect.

- You may have a Sales career, but your jobs would consist of admissions sales rep, pharmaceutical sales rep, and account manager.

So, you may be looking for a job, but that job needs to fit within the larger vision of your career.

If your jobs look more like pizza delivery person, project manager, sales specialist, IT helpdesk rep, and dental technician, then it is very difficult to find the theme or trend and identify your career. Make it very easy on your employers and start your path toward a career that you love.

Application Tips:

- Don't get so caught up in your job that you lose sight of the big picture of yourcareer! Stop just going through the motions and ask, "Where am I going. Is this job leading me to something more?" Refer back to your Career Plan.

- Know how you impacted your business! What likely fell apart since you left?

WHAT WORK IS IMPORTANT TO YOU?
DAY 7

Bottomline: You won't give 100 percent to work that is not meaningful to you. Several years back during my time as an engineer/program manager for a global semiconductor manufacturer, I found myself not caring all that much about the products I was supporting. In the great world economy, it was important, but to me, I probably could not have cared any less if future cell phones could toggle between portrait and landscape mode simply by rotating my phone. That was the nature of what I was bringing to life, and I simply didn't care about it.

As I look back, I was rarely energized to do the work. I was excited by the magnitude of my impact. Ensuring production readiness for multimillion-dollar change programs seemed very important, but the products themselves were nothing to me. Whenever I had lunch with my teammates, I preferred to talk about anything except work! I enjoyed talking about my kids, weekend plans, anything other than the projects, engineering resources, or our overseas factory capabilities. And as the workload grew, my interests waned. As more of my personal time was demanded for this work, I started to question my motives. I mean, my paycheck was fantastic, nearly six-figures, but could I continue to give into something just for the money?

It wasn't until later when I started my career services business full time that I began to notice an awakening in me. I was really making an important difference in the lives of people, and I could see it!

I'm not saying that semiconductors don't matter and the work is boring. Rather that it wasn't important to me. You must do work that means something to you or eventually you'll find it nearly impossible to give 100 percent, show up with the right attitude, and stay energized to give the company your best.

Application Tips:

While it is wonderful to appreciate what you have, how many people will you truly impact if you are miserable where you are? Being in a place where you thrive will bring appreciation, recognition, and pure joy.

- How are you wired? For example, I know that a credentialed electrical engineer can tell several details about a device from the way it's wired. Similarly, how are you wired? What things anger you? What connections do you make consistently? What excites you? Through what lens do you see the world? What has colored your view of the world?

_____

_____

_____

_____

_____

_____

_____

_____

WHAT REALLY MATTERS TO YOU?

DAY ⑧

On Day 4, we talked about having high expectations from your work. Now, let's go a little deeper. Most applicants and candidates don't realize that they should be getting as much from their employer as the employer gets from them. Here are some specific questions for you to answer as you get ready to conduct your search:

- What functional position do you want to have (common job titles)?

- In what industry/industries do you want to work?

- How does this position help you reach your long-term goal(s)?

- What is your ideal commute time?

- Are you willing to look in other locations (cities, countries)?

- What work schedule do you need to have to accommodate your family's needs?

- What is your ideal salary range?

- What kind of company do you want to work for (aggressive sales company, employee-centric/family-oriented, international with opportunities for travel, government contractor, nonprofit, small, medium, large)?

- What are your biggest perceived barriers to entry (age, weight, ethnicity, citizenship status, lack of degree, lack of experience)?

- Are you willing to do what's necessary within reason to become qualified for this ideal role (willing to invest in a degree or certificate program, willing to take a class, willing to pay for a coach)?

It's not a hypothetical. You must have answers to these questions before you just launch your big career transition. Without your foundation, you may be tempted to spend hours customizing your resume and applying to numerous unrelated positions. Don't waste precious time chasing shiny objects. Use this information as the baseline from which you conduct targeted company research and make all application decisions. You will find more on company research in Section 2, Game Plan.

Application Tip:

Purchase or find a single notebook. Nothing fancy is required; a spiral notebook will suffice. This will be your job search journal and on page two, write your answers to each of these questions. Keep yourself motivated at all costs.

WHAT CHALLENGES ARE HOLDING YOU BACK?

DAY ⑨

I'm guessing you're like me. Whenever I'm getting ready to embark into new territory, I have a longer-than-desired period of fear. When I first stepped away from my corporate job to pursue my career management business, full time, I was too afraid to pick up the phone and ask for sales. When I was considering a change from one department to another within my company, I wasn't sure that I was qualified for the future role. When my husband had been fired from a job, he was unsure of how prospective employers would receive the news of his termination. The moral is that in hindsight, everything worked out just fine but those fears were real and legitimate concerns.

Take Fredrick*, he shared with me that he was interested in working for his county's department of corrections, but he was very nervous about a few things: (1) He was a large-and-in-charge man whose size could be quite overwhelming to some individuals, and (2) his father had previously been convicted of a felony. In addition to his size, Frederick was unsure how his father's criminal record would affect his candidacy as a corrections officer.

Regarding his size, I coached him on being the first to bring it up. He cleverly introduced the elephant in the room. Using humor and a proactive strategy, he was able to overcome that first hurdle. Now the fact of a convicted relative was a different matter for the criminal justice system as different states have different policies about this. Like always, with integrity being a central component to the code of ethics, telling the truth was a given, but only if the question was asked. Informed candidates know not to offer any unnecessary, potentially harmful information to their interviewers like chronic illnesses or bad habits. So, Fredrick decided not to mention it unless it was asked. In the event that it was brought up, Fredrick would simply place some distance between he and his father. "My dad is his own man who made his own decisions. My choice is to be on the straight-and-narrow side of the law and bring justice for the convicted." Something to that effect is what we practiced. Now, Fredrick was all set and had a plan to address both areas that had him feeling a little nervous.

Application Tips:

Ask yourself:

- What physical or emotional challenges do I have as I face this career transition?

- Is it doing me any good to hold onto these beliefs?

- Are these challenges even real?

- What will I lose if I continue to let these challenges keep me stuck?

- So what? How can I address these issues in a way that still show I'm a serious candidate and I'm definitely qualified for the job? You likely will need to rehearse responses so you're ready to address them if they come up.

DO YOU REALLY NEED TO GO BACK TO SCHOOL?

DAY (10)

So many career transitioners almost automatically come to the conclusion that they need to go back to school. While this may be essential for some it is certainly not the case for all.

If you are an executive who's risen through the ranks without a college degree, you may start to hit some serious roadblocks in your transition without those coveted letters BA or BS.

If you have been conducting a job search for longer than three months, and you're not getting any response then it may be time to do something different. Here is a checklist that will help you decide if you need to go back to school:

You need a degree if:

- Every job posting you're interested in requires a college degree.

- You are pursuing work in a highly specialized or regulated field.

- You have absolutely no experience or skills for your new industry.

39

- Your gut or spirit clues you in that a lack of degree is holding you back.

You may not need a degree if:

- Having a college degree is preferred, but not required.

- Experience is accepted in lieu of a formal degree.

- You have amazing, repeatable career accomplishments.

- You could earn a valued certification that would put you on a level playing field with your job search competitors.

Don't forget many reasonably intelligent people can see the equivalence of experience to a degree, so don't discount your experience. As a young, degreed electrical engineer, I was confused because here I was with this degree getting paid well while some technicians—who were far more knowledgeable than me—with no degrees were compensated a fraction of what I was paid. It can be that important so make your decision carefully.

Application Tips:

- If you have completed some school, but haven't earned your degree, include the degree information on your resume and parenthetically include "some coursework completed". This will help the Applicant Tracking Systems (ATS), the computerized resume scanners that search for keywords and phrases within your uploaded resume document, consider you a qualified applicant, and you will at least have the opportunity to wow your audience in an interview. I will explain more about ATS in the coming days.

- Do not limit yourself to entry-level roles due to this gap. There are plenty of quality professionals making meaningful salaries without college degrees.

HOW BADLY DO YOU WANT IT?
DAY ⑪

I talk to "serious" career transitioners all the time. My phone rings and the first thing I hear is, "How much does it cost to have my resume written professionally?" My instinct says— internally, of course—why does it matter what it costs? You know you need it, and if you give 100 percent, then it will completely pay you back within your first few paychecks. But still they resist.

Juanita*, one of my prospective coaching clients, was so desperate to get out of her current job. She had completed two master's degrees and was a very talented engineer. When I looked at her resume, I saw many of the same mistakes that most job seekers make, such as no clear objective. Juanita was not positioning herself for any specific types of roles. She simply offered a list of her job responsibilities and her schooling pursuits. This landed her several temporary assignments, but she was not having any significant success landing a meaningful, career-related role. Juanita was very emotional and even cried at how badly she needed out of her current situation, but apparently not badly enough, since at the first mention of monetary investment she went running for the hills.

I offer this example to force you to start thinking about how badly you want your life to change. If you're unwilling to do any of the following, then you may inadvertently be accepting a long job search, because it's not easy winning if you're only willing to do the bare minimum.

Are you willing to:

- Invest in professional services (resume development, job search/interview coaching)?

- Invest in quality networking events?

- Invest in professional development organizations?

- Actually attend networking functions and not come up with some last-minute excuse not to go?

- Talk to people about what you need?

- Ask your network for help?

- Do the work, and not just rely on others to get it done?

- Spend time every day to execute your action plan and not allow other stuff to consume all of your time, especially trivial stuff like Facebook?

- Follow up with people by phone and email—more than once, if necessary?

- Participate in your online reputation management, including spending time on LinkedIn and other professional network-building sites?

Application Tip:

Take the time to look at the list above and honestly answer each question. If any of the answers are no, you are not ready to tackle a serious career transition. It takes work to be successful quickly, so don't get yourself all excited about something you'll never realize for lack of effort.

NARROW DOWN YOUR TARGET COMPANIES
DAY 12

In her book, Successful Women Think Differently: 9 Habits to Make You Happier, Healthier, and More Resilient, author Valorie Burton talks about how having too many choices can leave you feeling powerless and buried beneath the weight of choice and paralyzed to move forward.[3]

Most career transitioners see this overabundance of choice manifest itself in the area of job boards. They are so afraid to draw their line in the sand and declare that they will only pursue a specific type of position. So when you hear of career transitioners applying to 100 jobs every week, these are what I call serial applicants (in the spirit of one of my favorite shows Criminal Minds). They will apply to anything that sort of looks good, and in the end, they usually find themselves drenched in a familiar misery—a boss who doesn't understand, a team they simply don't mesh with, and lackluster work performance.

A solution to this diagnosis is to target companies versus jobs. Imagine a search that only consists of companies you've already researched and confirmed has a culture that is consistent with your values. They create products or offer services that you actually care about. You won't spin your wheels interviewing like crazy only to find out that you're talking to start-ups when your plan was to pursue employment with established firms. Or how about you really want to work in high-tech sales, but you're applying to anything with sales in the title including pharmaceutical sales, which is very far off from high-tech sales? Don't waste precious time pursuing anything when only the very specific will do.

Application Tips:

- Make a list of at least 10 companies that you can legitimately see yourself being employed by. Start by typing in a search string in Google industry name+"companies"+city. Or you could check out Reference USA to research companies that match your industry preferences. This service is free at most U.S. libraries.

- Once you have your list, you will research each company one by one. Scan their websites and visit Glassdoor. com to see what past and current employees have to say about working there. Search for news positive and negative mentions and talk to your LinkedIn network that may be employed there. Ask your connections what it's really like to work there. This is an invaluable source of raw truth about your next possible employer.

DON'T JUMP FROM THE FRYING PAN TO THE FIRE
DAY ⑬

So you've done all that research on the Internet and have figured out exactly what career direction is in your future. Yes! You are on a roll. The only problem is the Internet doesn't tell you the whole story. Even Glassdoor.com can be a little one-sided as there are plenty of disgruntled ex-employees readily offering their bitter, less-than-positive remarks.

To avoid another potential employment disaster, a great proactive approach is to conduct informational interviews. During these exploratory conversations, you can obtain real information from real people who actually work in the companies you're considering. Remember my hubby who was terminated from his job? Well, he was so desperate to land something else that he bypassed all of these strategies. Guess what. He's miserable! That's right, he was so focused on the really-close-to-his-old-salary offer that he completely ignored the fact that he didn't enjoy the work. He was so used to being active, walking the floor as a supervisor in a collection-centric role that now as a customer service manager he was more frequently at his desk and due to the nature of the work, was forced to be more reactive, so the work wasn't energizing him. After only 45 days, he was already well past ready to move on. Don't let this be you.

Application Tips:

Hold one to three informational interviews with current and past employees at each company you are targeting.

How to ask: I'm exploring some career opportunities at _____ _____, I heard you serve in a _____ role and I would like to speak with you for about 10 to 15 minutes to get your perspective on the culture of the organization. When can we schedule a quick chat? Wednesday mornings are generally good for me.

Who to ask: Schedule your time with current employees of the organization and very recent, former employees. Make sure you talk to multiple past employees so you're not getting a single, potentially tainted data point. If you have a great relationship with the individuals, this is the best possible scenario.

How long should they be: Your interview should be brief and last no more than 30 minutes. Make sure you stick to the amount of time you requested.

When in the process do you schedule the interviews: After you've narrowed down your target companies and your resume is in the ready-to-send state, then you can reach out to request these informational interviews.

How to stay on track: When you initially reached out, you asked them for their perspective, don't change your tune and start asking them for jobs now that you have their attention. Limit your questions to discovering what you need to know. You may ask, "Whom else do you suggest I speak with?" Otherwise, avoid asking for a job with this group.

A layoff is not generally the best time to attempt a massive career change. The primary goal of an informational interview at this stage is to get some inside insights into a company's culture. If you are pursuing a shift to a new industry or profession, then the informational interview becomes absolutely imperative to make sure the grass really is greener.

BET YOU CAN'T PICK JUST ONE

DAY 14

It's true for potato chips, and oftentimes it's true with career paths. We are open to exploring multiple careers. It's not enough to say I want to be a salesperson and nothing else. You want to remain open to other possibilities. As I warned about earlier in this book, having too many options usually leads to paralysis, but narrowing down your career directions can leave you feeling empowered.

For instance, Dee*, when we worked together, she had been a successful insurance claims team leader for many years, but she wanted something more. She was OK with staying in the insurance industry but also wanted to explore other fields like oil and gas and promotion opportunities. With her, we simply created multiple versions of her resume, one to reflect each of her diverse career aspirations. Note: This approach only works if an individual would be completely happy with landing either of their career choices. If it must be a hybrid opportunity, then they must continue to trust the process until they land in their ideal space.

If you are not committed to a single career trajectory, then following these tips will keep you focused and continually moving toward something that's meaningful to you.

Application Tips:

- Identify your top two or three possible career paths

- Create multiple resumes, one for each career target. The content of each resume will be about the same; the major differences will be in the headline, the key skills you choose to emphasize, and applicable education and involvements.

KNOW YOUR WORTH

I can't tell you how many times my clients come to me frustrated because they just finished their MBA or PhD and they're still earning the same income. Or the number of folks who reach out to me because they want to make $30,000 more per year but have no experience in their targeted area. The bottomline: You must understand what the market will bear for your skill set and credentials.

First, let me make some things very clear to avoid any confusion.

- Advanced degrees do not always turn into more money for you!

- A PhD in a declining industry may not bring the extra dollars you expected.

- A $50,000 salary in Phoenix, AZ, may not translate directly to $50,000 in Boston, MA.

- If opportunities in your field don't exist in your area, you may need to consider relocating.

Hopes, expectations, wants, and desires all mean nothing without data to support them. Have you done the research to support your theory that a doctorate holder should earn $75,000 in the elementary education field? Has any data supported your claim that an MBA without actual experience should generate an additional $40,000 in income for you, this year? Did you compare cost of living indexes for your current location versus your new, future geography? Most people don't, and then they get sticker shock when they begin to receive formal job offers. It doesn't have to be this way. Make sure you understand your projected earning potential before you invest tens of thousands of dollars into advanced degrees and relocations.

Application Tips:

Visit the following websites and conduct your own salary research. It's your job to know!

- http://www.indeed.com/salary
- http://www.bls.gov/
- http://www.salary.com/

Check out their cost-of-living wizard if you're relocating

- http://www.payscale.com/

NOTE: Advanced education and credentials alone may not merit an increase for you. If you're not an awesome employee, deserving of greater reward, it may not come to you! Perceived worth and market value may be two entirely different numbers!

WHAT ARE YOU WILLING TO LOSE?
DAY 16

We live in a world where having more means you're doing better. More income means you're great at what you do. More material possessions are indicators that you're highly compensated and rewarded. But what about the reward of a truly fulfilling career?

You went to school, studied hard, and invested many years into a career that you now have come to strongly dislike and on top of that, you've just been handed your pink slip. What's a professional to do? It's not so hard, but as you embark upon a new career journey, you do have to wrap your head around a few thoughts first!

Is Money Your Real Motivation – Some people are purely motivated by income. Although this is rare, some people have mouths to feed and as much as they would love to change careers and be more satisfied with their work, they feel stuck since there are other people depending on them to survive. In this case, try to hang in there until you can identify a blended career that would give you the best of both worlds!

Can You Live on Less – If you're anything like me, it seemed that all the jobs I would have loved to do, made far less than my engineering profession. I was never truly OK with taking

54

a 50 percent reduction in pay until I had no choice. Then, I actually realized I was happier and life turned into a new adventure of repair versus replace, and my inner MacGuyver started to show. Duct tape could be seen on many broken surfaces throughout my home, and I wore it like a badge of honor. This momentary step back in pay may put you on track to more satisfying and lucrative opportunities.

Does it Make Sense – If the profession you are considering would put you squarely below the poverty level, then take some real time to consider this move. Unless you have a Trust fund to rely on, then you need to pursue careers that will realistically help you meet your financial obligations. If your mortgage is $2,000 per month and your new salary would be $2,500 per month, then you cannot still afford groceries, utilities, and the fun things that you've become to which you have become accustomed. Simply put, if your new career would certainly force you into debt, then re-think your strategy.

What would the Jones' Do – Don't even worry about them. They will always be around. The Jones' will not give you satisfaction in your career, bring peace into your home, or help you fulfill your God-given purpose on this Earth. So forget about them, swallow your pride, and focus on your health, your contributions to society, and how you can best bring joy into your home while being fulfilled at work.

Application Tips:

- Are there things you liked about your job? Write them down and capture the best elements of what you want.

- Evaluate the income reality and the income potential for your newly targeted career path. Make sure it passes the common-sense test. If so, go for it!

- Check your pride at the door. Truly ask yourself if your pride standing between you and a true life of career satisfaction. If so, you know what to do.

THE MONEY CONVERSATION
DAY 17

I am a huge fan and follower of financial guru, Dave Ramsey. I particularly love how he makes everything so simple. He even calls his Financial Peace University™ process, Baby Steps. Mr. Ramsey suggests that in order to gain financial independence, we must tell our money where to go instead of looking back over the month trying to figure our where our money went.[4] As a professional in the midst of career transition, money is a very hot topic and I would be remiss to leave you empty-handed on this topic. Let's address money from the how-do-I-survive-this-transition perspective and the what-expenses-should-I-expect-in-order-to-accelerate-this-season point of view.

When you're in survival mode, it may sound like common sense to cut off cable and start clipping coupons, but the reality is that you have become so accustomed to your lifestyle, and in the midst of all your emotions, you want some level of stability and normalcy to remain in your life. I offer instead of cutting stuff out completely, see how you can reduce your costs. If you can't bring yourself to cut the cable off completely, downgrade instead or just get a Netflix account so you can stay somewhat connected to your favorite shows.

Some of the expenses that you should expect and plan for are networking events, transportation costs, career coaching (resume development, professional branding), and a decent pair of shoes and tie (for the gentlemen of course). It can be tempting to eliminate career coaching or convince yourself it is not needed, but if the last time you learned anything about a resume or job search was five-plus years ago, then you need a coach. Far too much has changed in the job search arena to rely on outdated information. Not to mention, since you are unemployed, career coaching is a tax-deductible expense.

Finally, create a networking budget! There are several worthwhile events and activities that require some investment to attend. If you limit yourself to the free stuff, you'll also limit the type of folks you have access to! About $20 to $50 per month should do. This can be used for taking contacts out for coffee, lunch, or registering for networking events and meetings.

Application Tips:

Investigate possible cost savings in the following areas:

- Auto insurance - Ask about obtaining a rate reduction since your commute will be momentarily decreased.

- Cable / Internet - It can't hurt to ask if they're offering any specials. Let them know your situation, they may be able to offer $10 to $20 off your bill for a specified time. Also, see if they can temporarily suspend your services.

- Power - Inquire about time-of-use savings or budget payment plans. If you have a steady payment history, you are more likely to qualify for special programs.

- Food - Make grocery lists and meal plans. Purchasing enough food to cook for yourself and your family can be far more cost effective and nutritious than constant eating out.

- Medications - Ask your doctor for samples and generic prescription options.

Other considerations:

- Increase your income - Take a temporary or part-time job.

- Use your severance - Pay future expenses for your necessities (home, car, electricity) and leave a cushion for unforeseen emergencies.

ARE YOU WILLING TO DO "WHATEVER" IT TAKES?

DAY 18

This is a story about ethics. At one of our annual Human Resources (HR) forums, one of the panelists mentioned how job seekers will deceptively embed excessive amounts of keywords into their resumes by changing the font color to white so they appear invisible. At first it may seem shrewd but it's really an attempt to trick the system (Applicant Tracking System) into thinking you're more qualified than you are. It's unethical. So is the use of agencies that can create fictitious backgrounds and resumes for you. They can manufacture completely new personas that present you as the best thing since sliced bread, the problem is that none of it is true.

I also can't tell you how many times I work with clients one-on-one who have copied and pasted their resume content directly from the Internet. "Well. it sounded good, so why not use it?" Because it will put their moral compass in a tailspin, that's why! Taking credit for work you never did just to gain an opportunity is pathetic at best. The people I'm talking to through this book care about their careers, development, and qualifications. They are not interested in looking good short-term at the risk of their career-long reputation. Examples in recent news showcase con artists who obtained esteemed positions only to have it all stripped away and their legacy forever tarnished due to the unsavory means with which they gained their positions in the first place regardless of the amazing work they were able to accomplish.

Most of those same copy-pasters I've worked with have later come to realize that they could stand on their own merits. They just needed someone to help them see their own value, perhaps a mentor, an outplacement consultant, career coach, or even an old boss. The people you work with can oftentimes see you differently than you see yourself, so soliciting outside perspectives can be invaluable to your self- perception.

Application Tips:

Review your resume in its entirety and make sure you can personally account for every detail on it. If not, it's time to remove anything that you cannot support with an example.

TEST THE WATERS
DAY (19)

This book isn't only about getting back into the workforce following a layoff, it's also a career management tool that will help to keep you in position for amazing new opportunities down the road. One statement that still rings true is that you'll have an easier time finding employment if you're already employed. Let me tell you a story that supports this claim and how Deidre* used this to secure a major promotion and salary increase.

Deidre* is an architect who had started to believe she was bumping her head against a glass ceiling. She was ready for additional responsibility but felt like her current employer wasn't receptive to her yearnings for more. She was gainfully employed when she reached out to me to update her resume. (You see updating your resume isn't just something you do when you're between jobs.) She wanted to validate her value in the marketplace, so she—now armed with her newfound confidence on paper—"put herself out there." She submitted a resume to two firms that she had been eyeing and received immediate responses from both. As you can imagine, her confidence was now through the roof!

Now knowing that people were hungry to bring her talents

into their agencies, she was emboldened to approach her current management team and make some requests. She tactfully communicated what she wanted and expected: a salary increase and more leadership responsibility. Guess what. She got both within her current firm. She ended up not needing to go anywhere new. Deidre* was able to gain the growth and development she needed right where she was.

This is a great example of testing the waters and knowing what the market response will be to you. For you it may be posting a resume on Indeed.com and giving it a week to see what sorts of responses roll in. It may look like a career move that doesn't make sense on a linear scale, but it makes complete sense to you. Just like Peter stepping out of the boat and walking on the water, doing things in faith and making some bold choices to boost your own confidence will give you the nerve to dare ask for what you want.

Application Tip:

Test the waters of your industry or new career field. Do this by creating a new version or multiple versions of your resume, then post it or them. Your background may not showcase you as a perfect fit, but you'll never know until you try.

PLUG YOUR HOLES SO YOUR BOAT DOESN'T SINK

DAY 2.0

You've dreamed about career change, job change, and your return to the workforce long enough, and there are significant gaps in your resume to prove it. Spending all of your time dreaming leaves little time for action. Holes come in many varieties including experience gaps, employment gaps, and skill gaps, and I am here to tell you that if you don't plug your holes, your boat will sink.

Experience Gaps - You want to be a manager, but you've never managed. You want to be a consultant, but you've never advised or consulted on a project. You strive to be a senior team member, but your past history doesn't show a clear ability to make strategic decisions and influence others. You have experience gaps, and you must close them.

Employment Gaps - Six months here, two years there. It all adds up and what the prospective employers see is an unstable work history and red flags about your ability to keep a job. Employers see a lack of ambition and dedication to your craft and if your gap is recent, they see it is unlikely that your industry knowledge is current and applicable to today's marketplace.

Skill Gaps - Don't run away from schooling or professional development courses and workshops simply because it's been too long, they cost too much, or it looks too hard. Plugging your skill gaps can ultimately help to plug experience gaps. When employers look at a resume and see a lack of experience, but then find recent skill training in those core areas. They are more likely to overlook your experience gaps.

Application Tips:

- Plug Your Experience Gaps - If you're currently employed, ask for projects that will expose you to the experience you need. If you're not employed at the moment, seek out volunteer or internship-type opportunities that will allow you to gain the experience you need for your next career endeavor.

- Plug Your Employment Gaps - From this day forward embrace the concept that "looking for a job" is not an acceptable use of six months or longer. If you start to find your job transition taking much longer than six months, then start actively plugging your employment gaps with productive, skill-building, experience-building endeavors. Volunteering, interning, consulting, contracting, returning to school, professional development, blogging are all positively viewed activities that will take the spotlight off of glaring employment gaps. If you have past employment gaps, review your life and fill in some of your holes with the actual stuff you've been doing. But certainly, moving forward, don't rely on "job searching" as an employment gap filler. Creatively incorporate these items on your resume to show how you've spent your time.

- Plug Your Skill Gaps - Skills can be acquired through experience, training, and observation. Especially in our highly digital era, there are far too many opportunities available to have any excuses not to plug your skill gaps. There are free webinars, low-cost courses at your local community college, workshops offered through professional organizations, and classes offered at public libraries. Your task is to investigate them all and get busy participating in something that will teach you what you need to know and put you in position for the amazing career you want to have.

Goals – Recap

Knowing where you're headed is the foundation of arriving to your desired destination. Accelerating your transition back to work requires that you clearly communicate what types of work you're looking to perform. The clearer you are the better able your network is to help you. Now that you've got the eyes on your prize, you will outpace your fellow job seekers, who are merely looking for a job, not the job, by leaps and bounds. Revisit your goals and career objectives often and evaluate future opportunities against the plans you've coherently outlined for yourself. We're now 20 days into this 60-day journey and I pray that you're feeling confident and excited about conquering this job search now that you have a clear vision.

Part II – Game Plan

A 21st century job search takes real effort, and unfortunately few job seekers are willing to do what it takes to accelerate their job transition. Many people who find themselves suddenly unemployed celebrate by increasing their TV time. They often forget to exercise and take care of themselves because they are stuck in their emotional rut. Then, one day they decide they're ready to get busy, and they start submitting applications online, sitting, and waiting. This is not a strategy, but this next section will roll out some robust options to help you not only own this job search process, but to accelerate your transition and manage your career moving forward.

A genuine career search is not for the fearful or for easy quitters. It involves doing some things that may be uncomfortable—not unethical, but uncomfortable—such as embracing a lifestyle of networking, investing in yourself, and attempting other contemporary approaches, especially after you've seen that the old ways are no longer working for you. The list goes on, but the ones willing to do the work, get the prize.

The challenge is that so much has changed in the landscape of a job search from the time we learned about it in high school. We have not re-learned job seeking in the present-day time in which we live. Even without up-to-date knowledge expecting you to put one foot in front of the other without a roadmap would be unrealistic. This next section will help you in your quest and will answer various versions of the question,

"How do I do that?" Job search. Networking. Interviewing. It builds on the goals section so make sure you didn't skip that crucial foundation. I double-dog dare you to do the things outlined in the entire book, so you can begin to ooze success and acceleration in your job search. Ready. Set. Go!

YOUR RESUME IS NOT ENOUGH, BUT IT IS VERY IMPORTANT

DAY 21

In the U.S. business culture the term resume is often synonymous with job search. The moment you find yourself without employment, one of your first thoughts is "I need to update my resume." Yes! This is so true. But is your resume enough for today's job search journey? I say, "Absolutely not."

Nearly 98 percent of all modern employment recruiters are actively sourcing candidates on LinkedIn. We also know that upon receiving a resume or application for employment that most HR professionals and hiring managers are taking to the Google information superhighways to find other digital evidence of your professional existence.

Most major corporations even have an employee referral program, so don't allow yourself to believe that only having a resume will suffice in this cutthroat job market The new trend is to find a backdoor entrance into the company of your choice, but if you are the lone wolf, blindly sending out generic resumes, none of the decision makers will ever know who you are let alone vouch for you to be brought into the organization.

There are all sorts of new approaches to earning the attention of referring employees, hiring managers, and recruiters, and you must start to implement some if you expect to see accelerated results. Here are a few:

- Build and manage your online LinkedIn profile

- Participate in group discussions within LinkedIn

- Join a professional development organization

- Blog and follow other industry experts

- Comment on industry thought leaders' articles

- Leave your house. Attend at least one networking event a month and create solid relationships

- Pick up the phone and call former contacts and colleagues

- Volunteer in the area in which you are wanting to engage

- Use social media to get the word out that you could use job search help. If they don't know what's going on they certainly won't be able to assist.

Application Tips:

- Pick at least two of the above strategies and choose a single day each week to implement them. Allow one to two hours on your daily calendar.

- Check out many of the well-vetted resume development books and make sure your resume is ready, because while your resume is not enough all by itself, it's still very important and you don't want your strategies to break down because you offer a mediocre portfolio (resume, cover letter, LinkedIn profile).

- Check out my ebook, Your Resume is Not Enough: How to Network Your Way Up the Corporate Ladder that is available at www.pinkslipcrush.com.

Understand the role of your portfolio:

- Your cover letter's job is to garner attention for your resume and online presence.

- Your digital footprint and resume's job is to pique employer interest enough to invite you for an interview.

- Your job in the interview is to find a fit with an employer and for them to find value and chemistry with you.

THE 5 STREAMS OF JOB SEARCHING

DAY 22

As an entrepreneur I've often been taught about the importance of having multiple streams of income. This way, if one area of my business is underperforming other areas can compensate. The same is true during your job transition; you can't put all of your eggs in a single basket, cross your fingers, and just hope for the best. That's not a strategy. Here is a more in-depth look at some of the specific elements mentioned earlier that you can add to your job search today!

Job Boards - This is the most common strategy adopted by job seekers. The first task transitioners think to do is update their resumes and apply to jobs via search engines (careerbuilder.com, indeed.com). While these can be successful, they can no longer be the only way to find your next opportunity.

Leveraging Your Network - This may mean reaching out to your professional network on LinkedIn (more to come on this later in the Game Plan section) or getting out of your house to meet fresh, new faces that could possibly turn into golden connections for you. You can do this through job clubs and professional organizations.

Working with Recruiters - Recruiters generally want to work with people who are clear about what they want and are performing at the top of their game. Recruiters are generally paid by employers to scout top talent so if you're asked to invest in their services, do your research and get a second opinion. Another trick is that recruiters prefer to work with candidates who are currently employed, so you'll need something to bridge your employment gap. Take on a related volunteer role (volunteermatch.org) or put in for some temporary or contract assignments. This way you're keeping your skills sharp and remaining appealing to recruiters. If you're not having success in this area, your resume or presentation could be holding you back.

Using Social Media - For some of you this will mean blogging, but for others it will mean you're sharing and commenting on interesting articles written by others in your field. But for no one does it mean using vulgar language or coming across as uneducated. If you know that spelling isn't your forte, then run your social media posts through a spell checker. If grammar isn't your strength, then keep your messages simple to avoid grammatical pitfalls. And whatever you do, don't engage in highly galvanizing conversations about politics.

Managing Your Career - Really start taking an interest in your career and industry. When people know that you know your stuff, they take you very seriously. You'll no longer be willing to accept any old entry-level job. You'll be thought of first when the right opportunities become available.

Application Tips:

- Network - If you keep relying on the same network you already have, you'll likely continue to see the same results you've already achieved. You must expand your network if you are to expand your possibilities.

- If your employer sponsored outplacement services to you, be sure to tap into this resource. Even if they provide bare bones services, you will be able to pull from their resources and possible employment connections. Don't discount this!

CREATE DAILY ROUTINES THAT WORK
DAY 23

During my transition, I found it especially difficult to feel proud of myself when I wasted so many of my days on the couch in front of the TV eating less-than-ideal foods. I don't know how to explain it except to say I was definitely in a funk. It felt as if lead was weighing down on me, or an anvil similar to what used to fall on Wile E. Coyote's head. I can't properly describe it, but I know it was a real struggle to pull myself up everyday. Like I said before, this went on for several weeks or months before something happened that caused me to get re-energized and ready to push. For me, I honestly feel like the Lord God Himself pulled me out of my rut and reminded me to develop good daily habits so I could get back to work and be productive.

My new day was a stranger to the depression-filled days of the beginning of my transition. It consisted of tangible elements that would serve to thrust me forward in my quest for the next chapter of my career. Some of the components were:

- Get up and shower every day!

- Pick a location for the day (a place that would inspire me) it could be the floor, my desk, kitchen table, the library, or my favorite mobile office Starbucks.

- Create a meal plan that included at least some healthy options. No, I'm not a health nut, but I know that I feel better when I eat well.

- Exercise or get out of the house. Simple activities like playing a quick game of chase in the park with my kids or walking to the mailbox helped my mood. This also made sure I saw the sun regularly and replenished my Vitamin D.

- Take time to care for my home, because I work better in clean spaces.

- Apply to one or two quality positions, including resume and cover letter customization.

- Make one to two phone calls to connections, references, or follow-ups.

What does your ideal daily routine look like? Take a moment and apply the application tips so you can see a huge difference in your daily progress toward your big goal of getting back to work.

Application Tips:

Ideal work location(s): _____

_____

_____

Foods I will do my best to avoid: _____

_____

The number of resumes I will submit every day: _____

_____

Commitment to shower and look my best by this time every day:_____

Personal / Professional Development time: _____

_____

The number of follow-up calls and outreaches to make daily:

_____

_____

You may need a different version depending on the day of the week. But do have some structure built in so you can see a marked increase in your motivation during your transition.

DON'T ACT LIKE A POLITICIAN
DAY 24

How many times, around election season, do you receive those mailers with three bold promises from your local and national politicians? Personally, I take one look and throw them in the trash. They boast empty promises with nothing to support their claims. They may as well state they have the solution for world peace or world hunger!

What's wrong with statements like the following:

- I'll raise educational funding.

- I'm tough on crime.

- I'm on your side to improve our communities.

- I'll take a hard stance against corruption.

The problem is that they have no meat, no proof. Define "tough." We have nothing to quantify their statement. The same is true when you write generic bullet points and objectives on your resume without substance to back you up. The typical objective statement says something like "I am looking for a position where I can utilize my excellent communication skills and advance within the company." I can't even begin to tell you how outdated this is. And a common bullet point may read, "Managed projects for a Fortune 500 company," or "Answered 60 phone calls per day while treating customers with respect." My first reaction is, so what?

A great bullet point or introduction adds elements of "What's In It For Them" or WIIFT. Why should I care that you managed projects for a large firm when I really want to know that you did a good job, you achieved your targeted results, and that you did it according to the pre-planned schedule. So what you answered 60 calls! Were these complex customer situations that required delicate handling so you could retain a multimillion-dollar account? Did your peers only answer 40 calls? Give those supporting details so your audience will know the WIIFT. Value and proof are your key words here. What value do you bring to the table and how can you substantiate your results in such a way that they prove you've got the goods?

Application Tips:

- Scrub every bullet point on your resume and make sure it addresses the WIIFT factor. It should convey what you did, why it was special, and the impact it had on the company.

- Replace your I-focused objective with a You-focused value statement. Some have called this a profile or summary, but it will help you if you think of it in terms of a value statement.

- Begin each bullet point with an action verb (controlled,

delivered, designed) and the impactful result.

- Quantify as much as possible, especially critical for sales and consultants.

- Compare your contributions to others in the same position when possible.

- When it's not possible to quantify, then qualify, again tell why it was important to your organization, team, company, or industry.

- If possible, do try to communicate how you used certain tools, systems, or software applications to perform the task.

Address the Situation you faced, the Actions you took, and the Results you experienced (SAR format).

Common Usage	Preferred Usage (SAR format)
Performed A/R duties as requested	Completed a high-volume of A/R requests to increase revenues for the $10M business unit.
Managed a team of 7 engineers	Led a team of 7 highly technical engineers through concept, design, development, and testing of over 100 projects.
Sold products and services to various clients	Ranked No. 1 salesperson in saturated medical device sales market, surpassing revenue generation goals by more than 320%.
Responsible for new factory launch	Accelerated new, factory qualification by 12 weeks, through project leadership, in anticipation of capacity overfilling.
When you can't quantify...	Resolved irate, customer grievance by calmly educating client on win-win alternative solutions.

81

BRING YOUR RESUME INTO THE 21ST CENTURY

DAY 25

With plenty of excellent how-to-write-your-resume books out there, I will not delve too deeply into how to build a powerful, attention-grabbing resume in this book. Rather, I'll emphasize some of the most important elements that you'll need for your search. With that, we'll tackle the resume from top to bottom:

Contact Information - provide only one contact number, make sure your email address is professional (first name.last name@ email.com). There is no need to include your street address; your city and state will suffice.

Online Presence - Include hyperlinks to your relevant online portfolios like LinkedIn.com or other web-based locations to show your understanding of modern trends. This can indicate that you are flexible and open to change.

Objective - The objective has gone the way of the dinosaur; it's extinct. If you think about it objectives have always been very selfish and "I"-focused. But in the 21st century job market there are typically few jobs for hundreds if not thousands of applicants, so employers are not interested in what you want, rather what you can do for them. Therefore, your objective must be transformed into a headline, which clearly indicates your target position title and a short overview of your abilities and a snapshot of some of your most impressive career accomplishments. This may be called a summary or profile, but it's quite important for your contemporary resume.

Key Skills - This is a great place to list bullet points of the core skills that are required for your target positions, you actually possess, and you can demonstrate. This is where you will primarily focus your customization efforts for each unique position.

Order Matters - Placing the most important content first can make or break you. If your education is stronger than your experience, place it higher on your resume. If your degree is in engineering but you've worked as marketing specialist for the past five years, then your experience will outshine your credentials.

Experience - Be sure not to emphasize your titles and employers over your dates of employment. Right align work dates. Also, be careful to not merely list your job responsibilities but to spell out your significant accomplishments. Each bullet point should be special and should capture what you did, why it was special, and what impact it made to your organization, customers, or other stakeholders.

Education - Unless you attended a prestigious Ivy League school, your degree should be prioritized over the school. If you attended school but did not complete your degree program, use the format "Bachelor of Science (B.S.) in

Accounting (some coursework completed)."

Applicant Tracking Systems (ATS) - You may know of these, but perhaps not by name. When you hear of computers that scan resumes, it is in reference to ATS. Your resume must be formatted in a specific way in order for the right pieces to be picked up by ATS. They scan for keywords so it is very important that you use the terminology provided by the employer in the job descriptions. Hint: Those are the words and terms that will be scanned.

Application Tips:

- If you create multiple resumes for various industries or skill sets, the content of each resume will be about the same; the major differences will be in the headline, the key skills you choose to emphasize, and applicable education and involvements. You could end up with five or more versions of your document to suit all the variations of your chosen profession.

- For a great selection of resume books you can visit your local library.

- It is OK and frankly, encouraged to use up-to-date formatting techniques like shading and creative font choices. This serves to connect with the human, non-ATS readers.

WHAT'S YOUR 20?

DAY 26

Again, this book is far from your traditional job search approach. Most normal job seekers will "update" their resume and start applying to 50 to 100 jobs on job boards each week. But you are not an average job seeker, you are a well-equipped, confident career transitioner, and you have a secret weapon.

Now, I'm not altogether opposed to submitting applications through job boards, because occasionally they do work. I'm interested in helping you to accelerate your transition and elevate the quality of your results. As we discussed in Day 12, you should have a clear idea of what type of career you'd like to have and what your ideal salary looks like. But you do all this so that you'll be able to filter out opportunities that don't fit the bill. So, in addition to posting your resume to job boards, I also recommend utilizing the "20" approach.

Your "20" are the top 20 companies that offer the type of work you really want to and are able to do. The point is that once you have a targeted list of 20 or so employers, you're better able to focus your job search efforts in those areas as opposed to spending several hours each day in pursuit of opportunities that might work for you. This approach does take a little more time and effort but is more likely to produce a rewarding and fulfilling career for you. Give this approach a try and watch how much more productive your job search time will become. Instead of applying to five random jobs this week, you'll reach out to five specific people at your targeted companies knowing that your efforts are moving you toward what you really want.

Very recently, my wonderful husband who works very hard for our family found himself dissatisfied with his employer so he launched a job search campaign, and he soon started getting offers only to say, "I'm not going to take that one because there is no bonus potential" or "I like this one, but it's kind of far away from where we live." The moral is that he was wasting time interviewing and negotiating with companies he could've easily researched in advance and never agreed to interview with in the first place. Those fit items we discussed earlier in Day 8 are really important, and now they come into play so you can filter through the hundreds of companies in your area and focus on the 20 that are likely to give you what you're actually looking for.

Application Tips:

Once you identify your 20, you can follow them on LinkedIn and identify any common connections. Now you have an excellent starting point.

- Research at Glassdoor.com

- Search company websites and scan through press releases.

WHO'S ON YOUR SUPPORT TEAM?
DAY 27

Accountability is one of my absolutely favorite words in the English language. So as I ponder this word, which means, an obligation or willingness to accept responsibility or to account for one's action, according to the Merriam-Webster Dictionary, I wonder how many of you are using this often free tool in order to accelerate your career transitions.

As I look at this word a little more circumspectly, I see the opportunity for transitioners to accept responsibility for their actions and also for their inactions. Looking for a new job is one of the most daunting tasks imaginable, and it's easy to justify inactivity. It's just as easy to talk yourself out of doing the things you know you need to do, but are extremely uncomfortable. Here is an example of how accountability can work in your favor:

If you've been strongly opposed to attending a networking event, telling your accountability partner the time, date, and your expected outcomes will keep you intent on showing up. Inaction should also have consequences and are more likely to get you off your butt to take the necessary actions. Owing breakfast for each no show will generate a level of motivation at least for your wallet.

Sometimes it is difficult to select individuals who will actually hold you accountable versus letting you off the hook. A bad hair day is not an excuse for not attending a job fair. A headache is not a reason to miss an application deadline for the perfect position. You may choose a spouse, friend, mentor, or fellow networker. What's important is that you will need to share your written job search strategy with these individuals each week.

Remember at the end of the day that it is you who will suffer if you don't have a plan or if you don't stick to it. It takes courage and discipline to keep running your race until you win the prize, so I challenge you to reach out to someone that will truly make sure you're staying on task until the job is done. Doing the work is your job, they are there to support you, and be a firm reminder of what's at stake.

Accountability is an important facet of your support, but there are other dimensions to your success. You may need a cheerleader. Someone who encourages you versus checks up on you. You may need a confidante—one who you can vent to but they will help steer you back onto the course.

Application Tips:

- Identify one to two accountability partners, one to two cheerleaders, and one confidante. Then, call them and make sure they are OK with fulfilling their roles.

- Every Friday send them a weekly forecast of what you plan to accomplish and recap your results from the current week.

- Spell out your motivational statement with each individual (your why).

- Write down consequences for inaction. Tip: Financial penalties usually work well.

BUILD AND KEEP BUILDING YOUR PROFESSIONAL NETWORK

DAY 28

Many people hear the word "network" and they shudder. They envision a large room full of strangers shaking hands, asking others "so what do you do," and exchanging business cards. The concept of networking really gets a bad reputation among individuals who are looking to re-enter the workforce. Now, in addition to the awkwardness above you have to figure out how to explain that you're currently out of work and reveal the type of work you're looking for. This can be really uncomfortable if you're not prepared, but you will be!

I am proposing a lifestyle of networking. Far too often people will attempt to "build a network" once they've lost a job and while it's never too late to start building your network, it may severely slow your efforts to return to the workforce. And unless you want all of your future transitions to be longer than necessary, start building your network now and keep building it during your transition and throughout your entire career.

Doing things like calling just to say hello! Having lunch with your buddies. Hanging out for happy hour, even if you don't order anything but water, are easy-to-do examples of maintaining your network. Calling to say Happy Birthday. Sharing a great article or tip with someone in need.

Volunteering. Giving someone a ride. Attending an event, even if you didn't really want to, just to show support. Asking how _____ 's going (maybe they mentioned a project or opportunity). Sending a letter or card in the actual mail (not email). And of course, there are many other things you could do, but why not start here?

Networking is not always all about you and what others can do for you, but rather what can you do for others and meet their needs. Your efforts will generally be reciprocated when you have a need. So if you engage networking with a What's-In-It-For-Me (WIIFM) attitude, you will fail.

Application Tips:

For new acquaintances:

- Follow up within one day to one week of having met them.

- Send a custom LinkedIn invitation (results may be slower) and call them to find out more about them and have a conversation (faster results expected).

- Take cues from what they said or find common ground from their social media profiles and share something that is relevant and demonstrates your interest.

- Request a small amount of their time so you can get more information about where they work, but you are not yet cleared to ask about a job.

91

For existing network (this does not include people you are connected to on LinkedIn but don't really know):

- Inform them about your current job search and ask them if they can help (spell out specific helping options).

- Avoid trying to guilt people into helping you, i.e. "You remember when I helped you, now it's my turn to need help."

THE BLESSINGS ARE IN THE DETAILS

DAY 29

Whether you are busy building a network, looking for your next opportunity, or later, working on a job that you love, you will have to communicate with people at varying levels. While you're communicating, you can do so with excellence or with a bare-minimum effort. I will share two actual emails I received from job seekers and you tell me which one is better?

Email No. 1

Hello,

Hope all is well in your world and 2015 is bringing exciting successes both professionally and personally.

Have you been in this space recently? Then, you know what it's like, if you haven't consider yourself very blessed.

I am actively pursuing a new Best Opportunity, using all the tools in my bag of tricks and one of those is reaching out to my network, that's YOU!

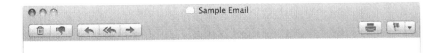

Here's you come in and   .can float my resume, offer up my name to a hiring manager, share a colleague's name who is interested, or point out a networking/relationship building event

- Any positions in your company where my skills would benefit?

- What about in your own professional network outside your company?

- Where are you networking?

- What have you found successful in your job search?

What do I offer?

- Solid project management that delivers on time and on budget

- Strong collaboration that gets everyone rowing in the same direction and gets things done

- Diversity across industries, technologies and disciplines

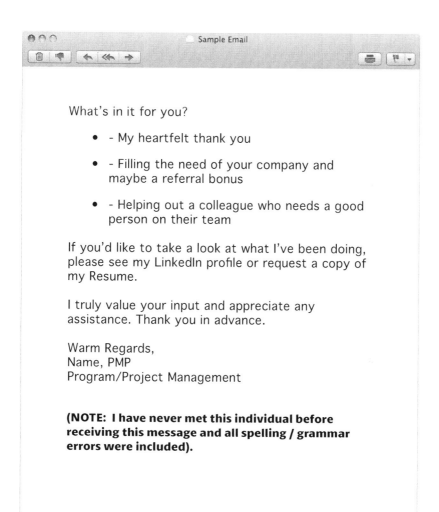

What's in it for you?

- - My heartfelt thank you

- - Filling the need of your company and maybe a referral bonus

- - Helping out a colleague who needs a good person on their team

If you'd like to take a look at what I've been doing, please see my LinkedIn profile or request a copy of my Resume.

I truly value your input and appreciate any assistance. Thank you in advance.

Warm Regards,
Name, PMP
Program/Project Management

(NOTE: I have never met this individual before receiving this message and all spelling / grammar errors were included).

Email No. 2

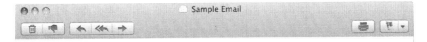

Dear Brenda,

I really want to thank you for becoming a connection this year. I have been blown away by the generosity and camaraderie of the résumé/CV writing community and the number of writers who come from upstate!

The month hasn't left me much time for meaningful work, but I wanted to take a moment to pause from the chaos to wish you all the best as you finish up 2013 and prepare for the start of another year. I pray that 2014 will be rich in opportunities and blessings for you, your family and your business.

My goal next year is to actually find ways of working with experts like yourself in the industry through subcontracting or other opportunities. If there is anyway I can support you in your work next year, please let me know.

Have a happy and safe holiday season and new year!

Warm Regards,

Name,
Career Professional

(NOTE: This was the third in a series of small-talk interactions following a personalized LinkedIn invitation request).

Everything from requests for informational interviews, LinkedIn invitation requests, interview acceptance letters, post-interview thank you letters, offer acceptance letters, letters of resignations, letters to your colleagues announcing your separation, or functional work emails are all important and can be strong indicators of your future success. You ultimately want to help and be helped. You don't want to send people running for the hills because you appear as though you can't spell. Who would be willing to vouch for someone who takes no pride in their first impression and enduring work?

So what happened? I ended up hiring the writer of email No. 2 to work on my team while I promptly deleted email No. 1.

Application Tips:

- Always spellcheck and proofread because spell check will miss words that are spelled correctly but are incorrect, such as from and form.

- Make sure you're message isn't totally self-centered. If you're so busy talking about what you want and want you want me to do, others are less inclined to help. As a reality check, count the number of times you use the word "I" in your messages.

- If grammar is not your forte, ask a well-versed confidant to review your communications before you send anything out. Don't use this as a crutch. Consider joining a group like Toastmasters or taking an English composition class at your community college.

- Be as concise as possible. Short and sweet are preferred over long and drawn out. Make your point very quickly.

- Always close with a call to action. What do you want them to do as a result of seeing your message? Call you for an interview? Call you for more information? Respond with their availability over the next two weeks? Give you the name of a referral?

- As much as possible, take the ownership off of them and place it on yourself. Anytime you're creating more work for someone else, the more you are creating strain on them and you will get further down on their to-do list.

- Allow yourself the opportunity to follow up by saying "I know you're busy, so if I don't hear back by _____ _____, I will plan to follow up personally for your convenience."

NETWORKING 101 – IDENTIFY YOUR NETWORK
DAY 30

We talked about building a network in Day 27. Now, I'll show you just how big of a network you probably already have. Think about your last few trips to the grocery store or mall or business function. Did you bump into anyone that you knew? Odds are you probably did. How about your last airplane trip? Did the person next to you strike up a conversation? Did it end with an exchange of phone numbers that neither of you ever did anything with?

Begin to embrace the lifestyle of networking and let's start by capturing the folks that are already in your power network. Hint: It's probably more than you think. Now, as you begin to understand where you'd like to work next, you can identify who your internal referral sources are. You have solid, warm introductions that can be made to decision makers in your field. You've been sitting on a gold mine and it's time to cash in.

Exercise:

For each group of people, write down the corresponding number of individuals and include a contact method for each person. Use a sheet of lined paper or print a free copy of a Network Builder at www.pinkslipcrush.com.

- Friend, family, and neighbors: List at least 30

- Former co-workers: List at least 30

- Service providers (i.e. Barber, stylist, grocery clerk): List at least 10

- Fellow parishioners: List at least 20

- Fellow volunteers (past or present): List at least 10

- NOTE: If you notice, you now have at least 100 people identified!

- Now pick up the phone and call each one or send an email just to say hello. Do it now, don't think about it or you'll end up continuing to do what you've always done.

Application Tip:

Make sure you actually write all these names down. If you find that there are people in your network that you need but don't have, this is the beginning of networking with a purpose. Who do you need to meet? How will you find and connect with them? Will you use LinkedIn? Are they going to be a meeting or presentation? Find out where they are, go there and meet them, then follow up after the fact to start building a genuine relationship, which you can later leverage once you've earned the right to do so. This is difficult to do, especially for the introverts among us, but this is the work that most professionals are unwilling to do and will set you apart.

YOUR ELEVATOR PITCH

DAY 31

Inevitably it happens. You are making an introduction and then come the questions: "So, what do you do?" Some respond by giving a job title or position title. However, a more savvy person actually tells what he or she does.

You may have been told at a career workshop to come up with some clever, well-meaning value statement to respond to this question. I offer a different way of thinking, and it involves plain English and non-flowery vocabulary. For example, notice the difference in the following two responses:

1. I change peoples' lives through artistic expression.

2. I get to help children express and resolve their emotional trauma through a fun, therapeutic process called art therapy.

The second response is generally more meaningful, because it clearly explains who you help, how you help them, and what your process is called. This answer is also referred to as your 30-second commercial.

However, whenever you're asked, "Why should I hire you?" you want to hit the inquisitor with a strong elevator pitch. This is also a great tool when responding to "tell-me-about-yourself" questions.

An elevator pitch gives a concrete, heavy-hitting justification for someone to really pay attention and consider investing in you. Imagine me driving the point home by banging my fist on the table. An effective elevator pitch has some degree of emotion attached. You are passionate about what's being said, so it will be soaked in authenticity. Here is my elevator pitch:

"Because you can't leave your career to chance. Working with a professional resume writer who's also a certified job search strategy coach can equip you to deal with all the career and job search hurdles that are certain to arise. They say, the average job transition takes six to 12 months, while my clients are only taking about two months. And with $20,000 to $30,000 salary increases being reported, can you really afford not to invest?"

Application Tips:

- Keep your elevator pitch and 30-second introduction to about 30 seconds. Much more than that and you may appear to be rambling and people tend to mentally check out.

- For your elevator pitch, think about why your prospect can't (or shouldn't be able to) live without you. Have prepared responses that answer why the company or client desperately needs your skills and expertise. Then, package it together into a succinct statement that will leave them wanting more.

- Be as specific as possible. Stating things like "I'm open to all sorts of opportunities", doesn't actually help your network make mental connections for you. Your words should trigger thoughts that lead to introductions and referrals.

BASIC TELEPHONE ETIQUETTE
DAY 32

It amazes me how few people actually know how to behave professionally on the phone. Employers are pickier than ever, and they will discount a candidate for the little things including your demeanor over the telephone. The following six tips serve to remind you of how important it is to be courteous and warm on the phone, but also give you some other considerations that you may have lost along the way.

1. No Desperation. If you've been out of work for a while and your phone finally rings, don't get so excited that the prospective employer is taken aback by your sheer enthusiasm. Now, I'm not saying it's wrong to be excited, but too much excitement can scare anyone away.

2. No Uncontrollable Environments. If you're out in public and you cannot control the noise level around you, it may be good practice to let unknown numbers go to your voicemail. You can always call them back, but don't ruin your first impression by asking them to repeat everything they've said because you can't hear them over a blaring announcement or screaming kids at the grocery store.

3. Voicemail and Ring Tones. Speaking of voicemails, leave a personal greeting so that employment calls can verify that they've reached the right person and so they can know you are articulate and can communicate clearly —a must-have skill for most job opportunities. Also, if you have a custom ring tone, make sure it's not offensive or contain vulgar language. If so, you can change it temporarily until you've found the position you were looking for. Lastly, it's so irritating when the voicemail has not been set up or the mailbox is full. Check your messages often so you don't run into these issues and stunt your job search progress.

4. If You Just Rolled Out of Bed. It's OK to give yourself a minute to refresh and perk up before answering potentially life-changing phone calls. To me there are few things worse than the scratchy, dragging sound of someone who obviously just woke up. If you receive that unknown phone call, go ahead and wash your face and get showered and revived before returning the call. Now, you will be on top of your game!

5. Pick One, Any One. If you know you're never home, why bother leaving your home number? If you know you can't answer your cell or if you regularly receive calls from unknown numbers (that you need to answer), then don't include your cell phone number on your resume. The moral of the story is if you can't pick a phone number for your resume, how can any employer choose which one to call? Make it easy on them and just pick one.

6. Smile; it's OK   Even though they can't see you, people know when you're smiling. They can feel it! I know that sounds weird but it's true. Try it with someone you know and ask if they can tell the difference. Smiling projects friendliness and a good attitude, which are pre-requisites for most professional opportunities.

Application Tips:

- Check your resume and LinkedIn profile to ensure only one contact number is reflected.

- If your voicemail greeting is a computer that recites your phone number, create a recording that includes your name.

- Practice a professional tone while on the phone with others. Even when you call to dispute a bill with a service provider a great attitude and professional demeanor can go a long way.

ASKING FOR HELP
DAY 33

My husband, who was a hiring manager for one of the largest banks in the world had been approached by a few job seekers hoping that he could get them back to work. What they didn't seem to understand is that just because they have an "insider" doesn't mean they shouldn't put their best foot forward.

Although my other half is more than happy to help people out, sometimes he can't because candidates have submitted poorly written resumes and many times they are not willing to do the work and be patient while the process works itself out. With this in mind, consider these tips if you are leveraging friendships and people in your network to help you get back to work:

1. Don't expect people to "hook you up" if you haven't put in the work. Take the time to put together a well-constructed resume and cover letter or letter of intent. Make sure to proofread for content, spelling, and grammar.

2. Mind your follow-up frequency. People that may have had every intention of helping you could quickly go running for the hills every time you call or email them

simply because you are too aggressive in your follow up. Remember their job is not only to help you get a job; they have company-related goals to complete, so be respectful of that. A good rule of thumb is no more than one contact per week unless you have agreed upon a more frequent follow-up schedule.

3. Have patience. Do not become discouraged because a week or two has gone by and you haven't heard anything from the company. It doesn't mean that your hope of working there is dead. Sometimes the application process can be several weeks in the making. I also recommend checking Google for recent company press releases. If the company is going through layoffs right now, then they may not be focusing on hiring new talent as a priority. Refuse to panic. Avoid calling your contact twice a day to find out what's going on. Desperation is not a good color on anyone.

4. Manners, manners, manners. I'll talk more about entitlement later in the book, but entitlement is the condition of having a right to have, do, or get something, according to Merriam-Webster Dictionary. When we walk around with an attitude of entitlement as if others are supposed to pass our resumes along simply because we asked them to, we'll be walking in the danger zone. You've witnessed it or you may have been guilty of it. It's fine to think positively and expect the best, but there is a very distinct line between faith and entitlement syndrome.

If you are guilty of violating any of these areas, not to worry, simply make an adjustment and continue working with your network in a courteous way so they can be happy to help you. They can possibly earn a referral bonus, and you can get back to work.

Application Tip:

Remember nobody has to do anything for you. People genuinely want to help, but if you project arrogance and an entitlement attitude, your network will leave you high and dry. People want to help you, not do it for you. If your contact asks you for something, don't throw a tantrum, don't complain, don't huff or puff, just do it. If you're not willing to do it, don't be too surprised when that connection doesn't come through for you. You drive the success of your career!

FOLLOW-UP ETIQUETTE
DAY ③④

Once you've officially applied for a position, how frequently should you check in to see if you were selected for an interview or a position? This is such a delicate question, but a common rule of thumb from career professionals is wait about one week after applying and after interviewing to inquire about a decision to hire or to confirm receipt of your materials. Thereafter, you should probably wait two weeks or heed what the hiring managers advise you to do. For example, if they say, we will be making our decision in two weeks, be sure to follow up in two weeks not one. The purpose of your call is to regenerate interest in you as a candidate. Also, smile when you talk so optimism will show up in your voice.

At a career event a few years back, I encountered this sweet, 50-something administrative professional. I offered her some suggestions to improve her resume and told her I would connect her with my husband once she made the changes. She implemented some, not all, of the changes. She called me twice in the same day and about three more times that same week to find out why my husband hadn't called back yet. Needless to say my husband essentially blacklisted her, and she never did get that opportunity, which would have been relatively easy with her inside connection. She overdid it, and many who are feeling increasingly nervous about their next paycheck may be tempted to follow suit. Exercise self-control during this transition process; it will serve you well.

Application Tips:

- At the end of each interview simply ask, "When would be a good timeframe for me to follow up and check the status of your hiring decision?"

- As part of your call to action, in each of your correspondences, include a statement that reads, I will follow up in one week to offer any additional information that may be needed. Note: You must create a corresponding calendar entry onto your scheduler so you'll remember to do what you said.

- Do what you said you would do. If you said you'd follow up in a week, make sure it's a week. People generally have a high tolerance except for excuses.

- Post-interview script: Hello, this is _____ (your name), I interviewed for the _____ position last week and I wanted to follow up and check the status of your decision-making process and see if any additional information was needed. I'm definitely excited about this opportunity and I wanted to thank you for your time. I'll check back in 2 weeks if I haven't heard anything by then. Otherwise, feel free to call me at (your phone number including area code). Thank you!

- Post-resume submission script: Hello _____
  (person's name), Thank you so much for your
  willingness to help circulate my resume within ____
  _____ (company name). I
  value your time and your confidence in my abilities. I'm
  very eager to hear something back, but I know you're
  busy doing important work. When you have a moment,
  could you please call or email me with any updates? If
  you need any other information, don't hesitate to ask.
  I'll get any needed information back to you within 12
  hours. Again, I appreciate your support and if it's all
  right, I'll check back in two weeks to see how things are
  progressing. Have a great day and please let me know if
  I can ever return the favor.

USING LINKEDIN TO REACH OUT FOR HELP, A 1-2-3. APPROACH

DAY 35

Over the years I have seen many different styles of outreach as we have all started to embrace this new, 21st century style of networking. Using LinkedIn was sort of forced on us whether we liked it or not and as a result, most professionals have haphazardly and rudely interacted with others. Clearly not everyone received the same courtesy training. There are some LinkedIn bulldogs who instantly ask for any and everything even from new acquaintances. But there are also extremely passive job seekers who never ask for anything and don't even fully realize that LinkedIn is intended to help you build a professional network so that you can tap into their influence when you need to. Where do you fall on the spectrum?

Regardless, here are some best practices to consider for using LinkedIn (or other professional outreach media platforms) as a tool.

1. Send an introductory mail

    a. Call out commonalities you found on their profile.

    b. Make sure it's customized. Don't try to rely on a generic, one-size-fits-all message.

    c. Show the WIIFT (what's in it for them) or why should they care about connecting with you.

2. Send a helpful piece of information (article, blog link)

    a. Once you know a bit more about what interests and needs your connection has, send appropriate resources as you encounter them. This is not to say that you have to spend an hour looking for things to send, but if you happen to see something show that you're thinking of them and forward it over.

3. Ask gently.

    a. Go for a small ask not a big ask, especially if you're not yet well acquainted.

    b. It's easier to ask for information versus asking for a job. Start with a request for 15 minutes of their time.

    c. You don't need to ask them to coffee, which takes far more than 15 minutes. You are looking for quality time to "pick their brains" and you can do that over the phone. You can go for a bigger ask once you've established real rapport with someone.

Application Tips:

- Set up an actual phone conversation with a person in your LinkedIn network to accelerate the rapport-building phase of your new relationship, so you can regale them with your awesomeness. Once they're personally convinced that you've got the goods, they may feel more comfortable referring you for internal opportunities.

- When evaluating the WIIFT think about if you're their colleague, their customer, their friend, perhaps you have a mutual acquaintance and it's a strong influencer. People generally want to help, but you have to help them understand why they should give their precious time to you versus the million other things going on in their lives.

MORE SCRIPTS FOR LIKELY SITUATIONS

DAY 36

Knowing what to say is often one of the most difficult things for job and career transitioners. Like I said at the beginning of this book, I want to make your search easier and give you a step-by-step practical guide. I would be remiss to try and accomplish that without word-for-word scripts you can use. Here we go:

Met you at an event

It was great meeting you last week at the _____ event. (Insert something specific you discussed). It would be great to chat a bit longer so I can get more information about what you do. I'll reach out and give you a call this week. Please let me know if there is a best time. Have a great day and I'm looking forward to reconnecting.

Your Name

Haven't heard back in over 2 months

It's been so long and I pray that all is well with you and your family. I had hoped to do a better job of staying in touch, but you know life gets in the way. Anyhow, I'm hoping to reconnect soon. I'm still actively pursuing my next role in _____ (your field here) and I appreciate your willingness to help with introductions and circulating my resume.

By the way, I heard you got a promotion (or insert other life event), and I want to hear all about it. I'll plan on giving you a call this week so we can catch up.

You've been invited to something that you can't afford

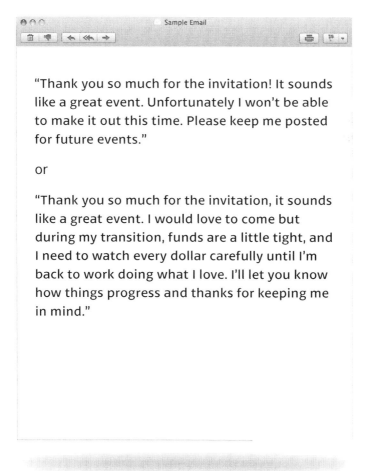

"Thank you so much for the invitation! It sounds like a great event. Unfortunately I won't be able to make it out this time. Please keep me posted for future events."

or

"Thank you so much for the invitation, it sounds like a great event. I would love to come but during my transition, funds are a little tight, and I need to watch every dollar carefully until I'm back to work doing what I love. I'll let you know how things progress and thanks for keeping me in mind."

By the way you don't owe anyone an explanation.

Application Tips:

- If you haven't talked in a while, put the ownership on yourself. Never blame or accuse your connection. It's not the best way to get people to help you, and quite frankly, it's rude.

- If you are invited to an event on Facebook, you don't need to go in depth with your explanation. A simple decline will suffice, but if you feel the need to explain, please don't include the fact that money is tight just stick with the first explanation.

POSITION YOURSELF AS AN EXPERT

DAY (37)

We all carry some level of bias around with us. It's up to us to sway our audience's perception toward the "us" we want them to see. In her book, Expect to Win, Carla Harris says, "If you think you can't change anybody's perception of you, you're wrong." She goes on to say, "You can train them to think about you the way you repeatedly describe yourself when you are around them and by consistently exhibiting behavior that is congruent with what you want them to think of you."[5]

A brand is what people think of whenever they think of you. It is, in many ways, synonymous with your reputation. So as a professional in today's marketplace, it is essential that you are communicating messages consistent with your brand. Bottomline: If I'm frequently receiving your social media posts and having regular exchanges with you, but I still have no idea what you do or what you can do well, then Houston, we have a problem. Think about it like this:

- Hairstylists – You would always want your own hair to look well groomed and offer easy styling tips for in-between maintenance.

- Golf Specialists - You may share the locations of the best greens, optimal swing stances, or instructional techniques.

121

- Financial Analysts – You may comment on money matters by Dave Ramsey or offer cost-saving suggestions that could be adopted by major corporations.

- Accountants –You may recommend income tax planning strategies and deductions.

- Engineers – You could share how technology is impacting us every day.

- Customer Service – You can talk about how to delight your customers and great success stories of customer resolutions.

Avoid bringing your strong political perspectives into your social media posts; if people disagree with you, it could be damaging to future alliances. What if you're a nurse and you're posting things that suggest you don't care about your patients and you just want to go home at the end of your shift? Now imagine that your boss is reading it and imagine that it's nearly performance review time. Now, you've got it!

Tread carefully, particularly since you are seeking new employment opportunities, potential employers and connections are watching. You don't know where your next opportunity will come from so don't burn bridges before you even cross them.

Application Tips:

- Showcase and protect your personal brand. Assess what you've been putting out there for others. Are you a chronic complainer or whiner? This will make people want to avoid you. Are you a positive influencer who is known for helping others? This will motivate people to want to help you. Know and understand how others have perceived you so you can do what's necessary to change their perception.

- Consider investing in a Reach 360 - Personal Brand Assessment. This is a 360-degree anonymous assessment of you. It may be a hard pill to swallow but if you're going to effectively manage your perception, you need to know what perception currently exists. URL: http://www.reachcc.com/reach/survey.nsf

WHAT'S ALL THIS ABOUT PERSONAL BRANDING

DAY 38

I've heard it said that a brand is more than a logo. It's also more than a title. It takes hard work, perseverance, authenticity, and patience to earn credibility and gain wide acceptance of your brand. Whatever it is that you'd like to be known for, start laying the groundwork little-by-little every day and show (don't just tell) everyone what you're made of and that you've truly got the goods. Enjoy your journey of building your awe-inspiring, moneymaking, true-to-yourself brand!

Here are some very specific things you can do to showcase your expertise to your audience(s) using LinkedIn. One feature you can use is LinkedIn groups. Here's how to leverage LinkedIn groups to help you build your personal brand.

1. Identify and join two to five groups that are related to your industry or the "thing/brand" you want to be known for.

2. Within those groups other professionals will be asking questions and making comments on subjects and issues that are relevant to that field.

3. Your job is to (1) post new thought-provoking questions and content within those groups and

(2) comment and participate in discussions that demonstrate your knowledge of the subject matter. Try to avoid simply agreeing with another expert. You'll want to pose your own opinion and insights to trigger new ways of solving real problems in your industry.

4. Be consistent, engaging, and active by posting in each group one to two times per week. You can start by setting aside 10-15 minutes per day, and this is very doable. Don't assume that your entire life will be consumed by this exercise.

5. Have realistic expectations. As I frequently mention, networking and building a personal brand is not an overnight thing. It is a long-term solution to help you get to where you want to be professionally.

You can see many of these strategies are long term in nature, which is why you cannot wait to build a network until you need one. If you don't start now, your next transition could take twice as long as necessary.

Application Tips:

- You can locate groups by typing keywords into the search bar at the top of your LinkedIn page.

- Select active groups only. If the last post in a certain group was eight months ago, then there will be no one there to listen when you post something.

- Look for groups with at least 200 members so you can

be sure to get a good variety of inputs and diverse opinions. Smaller groups can be valuable too as long as the participants are very active.

- Don't join more groups than you can actively manage, the key is to show up regularly so that your audiences can get to know you! Start with no more than five.

- Proofread your entries; you don't want to negate your expertise with poor grammar and spelling.

- If you're still not sure which group(s) will be beneficial to you, check out other people's profiles and see which groups they belong to. Start there!

READ! IT'S NOT JUST FOR 6TH GRADERS

DAY 39

Statistic Brain reported a shocking stat that 42 percent of college grads will never pick up another book.[6] Admittedly, I was one of those people. I always said, if the book is good enough, then it will be made into a movie. After being so hungry for new information and new perspectives for so long, I started to crave words. I asked a read-a-holic friend of mine how she's able to read so much with so little time in the day, and she said she always keeps a book with her, in her purse, in the car, at her bedside. That way, whenever she has a spare moment, a book is always within her reach.

One of the things employers want to know about folks who have been laid off is, how they have spent their time during the layoff. How amazing would your response be if you said, "I took a few classes and made sure I stayed up to date on the latest trends in our industry, and I read some books that really increased my understanding in the area of _____." Doesn't that sound better than, "I was spending most of my time looking for my next position"?

Now, I'm not one of those speed readers who can finish a 250-page novel in a night; it takes me some time. It's OK if you need a month or two to get through a book. The point is, find some books that will help you stay sharp, on the cutting edge, and remain competitive with what you know about the way your industry works.

Application Tips:

- Read for information - Once I recognized that reading non-fiction was critical to my career growth and later on my business growth, I knew it was something I had to do. If you are a fiction reader, at least add some non-fiction options to your reading list.

- Don't just skim - You can't effectively learn all the meaningful details if you're just breezing through the headlines. On the other hand, when you're looking for something specific, go directly to that part of the book read what you need and move on. I do suggest reading a little of what comes before and after for context.

- Don't just read books - For some of you (I'm especially thinking about engineers) it's difficult to find books that will sharpen you. Explore white papers and scientific journals. These definitely keep you in the know.

- If you're not sure what to read - Ask for recommendations from your colleagues. LinkedIn is a great place to post this type of question. Particularly in a LinkedIn group consisting of your industry peers.

5-MINUTE WARNING
DAY 40

It's amazing what you can get done in 5 or 10 minutes a day. We talked on Day 38 about creating daily routines that work. Well, it's quite easy to get overwhelmed at the mere mention of job search activities. Again, this book was written in digestible chunks so that your job search could be accelerated and your confidence would remain strong. With that said, let me show you how you accomplish all that needs to be done in about 5-or-so minutes:

So, if a typical day looks like:

- Exercise (0 minutes)

- Submit Applications on Job Boards (5 hours)

- Network (0 minutes)

- Follow Up (20 minutes)

- Time spent getting yourself motivated / Procrastinating (3 hours)

I propose the following to account for all the strategic elements of your job search

Exercise	15 minutes
Shower / Get Dressed / Eat Healthy Breakfast	45 minutes
Research Industry Articles / Browse LinkedIn Home Page (Like, Comment, Share)	10 minutes
Reach out to 3 LinkedIn connections / Send follow-up messages	10 minutes
Submit 1-2 Applications	2 hours
Lunch	1 hour
Personal follow up / build network	1 hour (whatever number of calls you can make in an hour)
Get out of your house and network or attend a job fair	2.5 hours
Pray / Seek God during devotion	30 minutes

Application Tip:

Today's tip is more of a commitment: A promise from you to yourself to adopt a new plan and stick to it even if it feels uncomfortable.

I promise not to allow myself to be discouraged. I promise not to allow procrastination and doubt stand between me and my desire to return to the workforce. I do have time to do all the productive things that are essential to accelerating my search and I will no longer rely only on the antiquated strategies I've been used to. From this moment forward, I will apply the modern game plan that I have learned to this point so I can do what I want on my terms.

_____

Your Signature Here

PARTNERING WITH PROFESSIONAL ORGANIZATIONS

DAY 41

One of the biggest propellers in my career has been my involvement in professional development organizations. As my pastor says, I stopped being a benchwarmer, and I got in the game. This decision was a catalyst for my professional growth. As you may recall, I was formerly working as an electrical engineer, but after my layoff, I chose to pursue a full-fledged career change. I accelerated my knowledge of the career services industry through participation in the Resume Writer's Council of Arizona (RWCA), Career Directors International (CDI), and The National Resume Writers' Association (NRWA). Over the past seven years, I've been consistent and active, and I currently hold leadership positions in two of those groups. One of which is a major, national, non-profit organization with over 600 members.

I can't testify enough about the benefits of partnering with organizations. Bonuses could range from referrals to innovative ideas, expansion of one's professional network, and exposure to otherwise unknown opportunities. We've all heard about the hidden job market and joining an organization has the potential of alerting you to those openings.

There are organizations for just about every industry and career imaginable so there are no excuses. Even if you live in a rural area, plenty of groups meet virtually so you're all set. And while there are some groups whose membership fees are sky high, there are others who are quite reasonable.

Application Tips:

- Research organizations (Use Google Search string: Industry name + location + "professional organizations", or, search in LinkedIn groups).

- Pick one or two organizations for your industry, preferably with a local chapter that meets regularly and attend one or two meetings as a guest. Before you join make sure you love the organization and that the members can actually help elevate your industry knowledge. Remember you've already set aside a budget for just such an occasion.

- Don't be a benchwarmer, get actively involved and support your new organization while they serve to develop you. Volunteer for committees, events, or leadership positions.

JOB FAIRS AREN'T WHAT THEY USED TO BE

DAY 42

If job fair attendance is part of your job search strategy, here's how you can make the most of them:

1. Find out who's going to be there and make sure they are companies you're interested in.

2. Apply online before the job fair, this is primarily what they'll expect you to do anyway so get a jump-start on things. This is a great chance to say, I've already applied; I'm looking for more information on the company and what it's like to work there. This way, you're starting to build rapport with the company representatives.

3. Make new connections while you're waiting in line.

4. Make recruiter connections with the specific companies on your 20 list. Ask if it's OK to connect with them on LinkedIn. Job fairs are prime hunting grounds for recruiters.

5. Follow up at least two times after the job fair has concluded. Follow up No. 1 is "nice to have met you and reminder of what was discussed." And No. 2 is "Hello again!" Then, reiterate interest in positions with call to action.

Application Tips:

- Attend industry-specific job fairs, this way at least you're standing in line for an hour for a job you might actually want! There's nothing worse than to finally get to the front of the line only to see that they are only looking for telemarketers to do some cold calling (and that's not what you do).

- Imagine, each employer talks to hundreds of job seekers during a job fair, make sure you have something unique to converse about that will make them want to remember you.

- Finally, show up with a few different versions of your resume ready to hand out, as you may want to be considered for a few different types of positions. But never submit multiple versions to the same company.

DROP IN AND SAY HELLO

DAY (43)

This is a story about a woman named Glenda, a wonderful, kindhearted person, but she found herself struggling to find her next opportunity. Until one day something in her heart told her to drop into a school and ask if they needed any administrative support. They said yes! She interviewed, and they hired her on the spot.

Now, while this approach is very uncommon (accept for entry-level retail positions), it proved to be quite effective for Glenda. The funny thing is before then I would generally advise against a door-to-door approach, but clearly there are some exceptions to this rule.

Sometimes all the planning in the world can't outdo a perfectly timed drop-in. Being in the right place at the right time can open even the most unexpected doors. This means you have to know where your ideal companies are and not be afraid to visit them uninvited. What do you have to lose?

Application Tips:

Incorporate this drop-in strategy into your game plan at least two days per month. It will change up the monotony of your routine and keep you on your toes. It's also a great opportunity to practice your 30-second introduction, and hey, you may meet a new golden connection.

Get your two days scheduled on your calendar to increase the likelihood of them happening. Plan to visit two to four locations during each of your outings. Write them here.

Week 1   Week 2

_____   _____

_____   _____

_____   _____

_____   _____

Week 3   Week 4

_____   _____

_____   _____

_____   _____

INTERVIEW PREP
DAY (44)

Preparing for an interview can be one of the most fun parts of this career transition process. It's exploratory, and you can really become convinced or turned off about certain opportunities. So whatever you do, don't skip this critical step and assume you can just show up empty handed.

Just recently, as I began my shift into providing outplacement services for people like you who were part of a corporate downsizing, I interviewed with a global outplacement firm, and of course, they asked me why I wanted to be in partnership with them. If I would have showed up void of a reason, I'm certain my window of opportunity would have been closed. But they were impressed and subsequently offered me a consulting role.

Some of the things I did in preparation were:

1. Google searched the company

2. Followed the company on LinkedIn to see what types of conversations they were engaged in.

3. Went to their website and researched financials, press releases, and mission statement.

4. Searched my LinkedIn network and found that I was connected to two individuals who worked there and I reached out to them for quick informational interviews. Both gave rave reviews.

5. Checked out employee feedback and salary ranges using Glassdoor.com, this way I could effectively negotiate any low salary offers and I could get more data points on the company culture.

Following these same steps will set you up for amazing interview success every time.

Application Tips

- Ask for the person's name you'll be interviewing with and research them on LinkedIn.

- Know your personal reason why you want to be there. This is different from understanding their mission statement. Think WIIFT and WIIFM.

- Take notes directly on your resume. Layout the job posting and your resume, side-by-side, and point out good examples to yourself. This can help a lot when your nerves get in the way.

- If your research leaves any holes, write them down and

ask those questions during your interview.

- Map out your driving route to ensure you know the best way and some alternate routes to get there so you're there on time, especially if you live in a major city with a plethora of traffic incidents. Become aware of road closures or public transportation strikes.

- Prepare for a phone screen. Quiet the room and your inner confidence crusher; have a go-to station that's already set up with pen, paper, laptop, and good cell reception.

HOW TO TACKLE INTERVIEW QUESTIONS
DAY (45)

I provide interview coaching to my clients all the time and I hear them say, "Boy! I wish you could just come with me to the interview. Just whisper those answers into my ear." And while I absolutely would if I could, I can't. So the next best thing is for me to provide them with strategies to help them answer the most popular types of questions. Here they are for your edification:

Tell me about yourself

Here, employers don't actually care about what you want (per se) but they want to know why you think you're a good fit at their establishment and what parts of your background are particularly relevant and exciting. They absolutely do not want to know how many children you have.

Why did you leave your last job? or Explain this gap in your work history

Stick to the facts. Don't elaborate or complain. Simply state the facts, steering clear of your opinion on the matter. For example, you can say, "I was part of a major workforce reduction," or "Due to the cyclical nature of our industry, a forecasted layoff hit our company and I was affected." Once you've answered the question, stop talking!

Tell me why you're interested in this position

This goes back to Day 43. You should have a personal reason you want to work there. It should extend beyond what's on the website. What is your personal connection to this company, department, or product line?

What is your biggest weakness?

Here you should only talk about something that you've already taken steps to overcome, or you may have already broken through. Never mention a weakness that's still a weakness. You could say something like " I felt out of touch with the newer word processing applications like MS Word, so I actually took a class at the community college, and now, I'm quite proficient." And never bring up a weakness that is critical to the position.

Tell me about a time when

This is where you will use the SAR strategy. SAR (S-Situation, A-Action, R-Result). Take a moment to think about an applicable scenario, then describe it using the SAR method.

For example the interviewer says, "Tell me about a time when you had to deal with conflicting priorities "

Your response: About a year ago one of our factories was destroyed by a natural disaster. Since this was our primary supplier, we had to quickly ramp up production in our secondary facility (situation). I pulled the team together, communicated the changes to our customers, and made sure the procurement team addressed all the contract logistics (action). Thankfully, all of our staff had been accounted for and we were able to meet our aggressive production demand without any business disruption (result).

What would you do if

These questions are designed to predict your future behavior. Do your best to think through all the possible angles here and answer as honestly and tactfully as possible. There usually is no right answer but do try to offer some justification around why you made your choice.

What questions do you have for me?

Make sure you actually have questions for them. Asking questions is a sign of interest. It's also an indicator that you've invested time in preparing for the interview. In addition to your specific questions about the company, consider these:

1. What would be my top 3 priorities once I'm in the role?

2. What do you (the interviewer) like most and least about working here? (This one reveals truth from the other side of the table).

3. How many people would be reporting directly to me?

Be sure to avoid potentially hazardous questions like

1. What is your drug-use policy?

2. What if I have a chronic illness, will I be able to take the time off that I need?

DURING THE INTERVIEW
DAY 46

You may not have interviewed in many moons, and it can seem rather daunting to remember all the little things you're supposed to do during an interview. I've attempted to make it easier on you, so you can focus on these six things:

- Ask if anyone needs a copy of your resume or cover letter (be sure to bring at least five copies with you)

- Smile

- Healthy eye contact

- Business cards from each of your interviewers so you can refer to each person by name

Provisions for your quirks:

- If you are a fidgeter, make notes to yourself as little reminders to stop.

- If you click pens as a nervous habit, tell yourself to stop.

- If you don't smile as a general rule, tell yourself to smile.

- Avoid discussing salary if possible. Allow them to make an offer before you begin to evaluate the pay.

Application Tips:

- When you receive business cards from your interviewers in a group setting, set them in the order of their seats so you can keep everyone's name straight.

- Also, tie all responses back to the reason you're there. If you're interviewing for a facilities management position, don't dwell on your academic credentials, which may have been in marketing. Focus on your relevant experience and situations.

- Another great use of the business cards you'll receive is to confirm the correct spelling and mailing addresses for your follow-up thank you cards.

- Bring your portfolio for note taking, pens, and your business cards. Silence your cell phone, not vibrate, silence. Wear a great business professional outfit and comfortable shoes.

AFTER THE INTERVIEW
DAY 47

Post-interview follow up is another thing that most job seekers won't do, and it will ultimately help set you apart from the others in the job search rat race. Again I say, be willing to do what most others are not.

Thank you letter - This can be a powerful way to express genuine thanks and to reiterate excitement and position yourself as a top candidate for a position. I don't believe email is a deal breaker versus handwritten notes, but so few send through the mail that it actually may work in your favor to go the road less traveled. Here are some scripts for you to use:

> *Dear Interviewer's Name Here,*
>
> *Thank you for your time today to review my credentials and culture fit for the Position Name Here position at Company Name Here. After careful assessment of my work ethic, skills, and abilities in the_____field. I do hope that you've found a match!*
>
> *I would like to reiterate my excitement about this opportunity, and I am confident to face the challenges that we discussed. Coupling extensive*

field experience, and excellence with your growth-focused environment seems an ideal fit.

I look forward to joining your team and learning of your decision. Thank you again for your consideration!

Sincerely,
Your Name Here
Your Phone Number Here

OR - If no response after a few weeks

Dear Interviewer's Name Here,

Thank you again for meeting with me a few weeks ago. I know you had planned to make your selection by now, and I suspect you're quite busy making this important decision. If you need any additional information, please feel free to reach out, otherwise I'll check back in a few days to request a status update.

I'm still extremely interested in the position and hope to hear from you with a positive decision. Thanks again, and I hope to talk with you soon.

Sincerely,
Your Name Here
Your Phone Number Here

References - I know you may have been accustomed to including the phrase "References Available Upon Request" at the bottom of your resume, but this is an antiquated practice. Trust me, employers know that you will provide them if they ask. The problem is, you likely don't have them prepared and you may not have spoken to your references in years. This list of references does need to be current, and it does need to have confirmed contact information available for each individual. Be sure to choose references that will powerfully advocate for you. As you are contemplating who these people could be, consider former bosses, colleagues, employees, customers, vendors, or other key stakeholders.

Application Tips:

- Thank you letter - Send this off by email or snail mail within 24 hours of your interview. Beyond 48 hours is far too long. Carve out time for this step as soon as you schedule the interview.

- References - Call the individuals on your reference list today! Make sure they still know who you are. Remind them about the work you used to do together and ask them if it's still OK that you use them as a reference. Giving them the heads up that they may be contacted will only serve to help you. The last thing you want them to say is, "Sally, who?"

- Also, for your references - Actually type up a list using the same document header as your resume. Include three to ten professional references. Note: sometimes personally references are requested, but not usually and for each one capture their name, phone number, title, company name, email address, and a one to two sentence relationship summary.

ACCEPTING AN OFFER AND DECLINING OTHERS

DAY 48

First and foremost, understand that companies can sometimes take months to extend an offer of employment, but when the offer does come in, how you handle it can translate into thousands of dollars in additional income.

There are several factors involved in making an offer: your experience level, existing pay structures within the company, the urgency of filling the position, and your ability to negotiate. A shocking number shared by my friend and colleague, Dr. Nadia Brown of Doyenne Leadership Institute, reveals that women leave about $700,000 on the table over the course of their career simply because they do not negotiate and ask for more. While this is not aimed at women only, make sure you're not on the boat that's $700,000 light.

While I don't believe that you always need to ask for more, you sacrifice your opportunity to complain later if you don't ask for what you want up front. Some offers are fair and some even exceed our expectations in the beginning, it's the low-end offers that we need to work with.

When the offer is too low - You need to know why it's low. After you've conducted your salary research (discussed earlier), you can now empirically rebut the initial offer. If you know the position, on average, pays $80,000 but you were offered $65,000, your response can be "Based on my research, I see that this position earns between $80,000 to $85,000, is there anything that can be done to pull this offer into alignment with industry standards?"

Try to avoid going first - You may be asked what salary you expect, and I want you to try and deflect as much as possible. You can try the old standby: "I'm certain that you'll make a generous offer in line with salary expectations for this role." But if that doesn't fly, always provide a $10,000 range, i.e. $80,000 to $90,000, that you gathered from your research. Don't ever just pull a number out of the sky. This number should be available from your interview prep.

If you need to decline an offer - Do so graciously. Every now and again they may find another great position for you in the company, one with a higher price tag. But if they don't, you won't burn any bridges by using the following script:

"Thank you for your offer of employment; however, I really am hoping to be compensated closer to the $90,000 to 100,000 range. Our attempts to negotiate have not yielded favorable, win-win results and that can happen sometimes. I do hope that you'll keep me in mind for other, more senior opportunities as I've really fallen in love with your organization. Thank you!"

Application Tip:

Pray before accepting any offer of employment, again, salary is not the only important factor. Make sure most, if not all, of your preferences are reflected in your decision. Consider vacation time, stock options, culture, telecommute options, flexible work shifts, and opportunities for advancement.

STOP TWEAKING YOUR JOB SEARCH TO DEATH

DAY 49

It is not uncommon for me to hear about job seekers who have applied to 100 or more jobs in a given week. While I'm vehemently opposed to this as a stand-alone strategy, I've also heard of seekers who have received dozens of pieces of feedback from a variety of sources, some legitimate and some who don't have a clue. Every one from your spouse to some so-called career expert has an opinion, but you must be very careful who you allow to dictate the quality of your portfolio.

When your resume isn't getting the desired results, the itch to make tweaks when some "expert" tells you to or when you're not getting responses from employers or recruiters is not always a favorable solution. In my honest opinion, tweaking your portfolio is different from customizing your documents for a specific opportunity and constantly tweaking your job search strategy can leave you without lasting impact in any given area. If you say, I tried the LinkedIn thing for a while and it didn't work, you would mistakenly draw the conclusion that LinkedIn is not effective. LinkedIn was never intended to be a magical job search solution; it is a long-term strategy component, so if you only give it a month to prove itself, you'll believe it failed you.

Some other mechanics I want you to watch out for:

- Voicemail greeting - Make sure it's professional and contains your name with your voice. Don't rely on the robotic iteration of your phone number. Employers may wonder if they've reached the right person.

- LinkedIn profile heading - Change your LinkedIn profile heading from "Currently seeking new opportunities" to " _____ Specialist Excited to bring leadership to $10M+ accounts." or something like that according to your actual field. Again, focus on value that you bring to the table.

- Your image - The image including your picture and your tone of voice and language choice can make or break you. If you're using a selfie photo on your social media profiles, expect some prospective employers to be turned off. Invest in a professional headshot or at the very least have someone else capture your headshot in front of a clean, plain wall.

Application Tip:

You may need to eliminate the second-guessing and invest in a consultation with a credentialed specialist (some acceptable accolades are CPRW - Certified Professional Resume Writer, CJSS - Certified Job Search Strategist, CCM - Certified Career Master, or an ICF certified Career Coach). This way you have confidence knowing your portfolio and job search game plan is effective, and you'll know the exact changes you'll need to make one time. You can of course contact the team here at Push Career Management directly for this or you can browse the hundreds of qualified professionals at the National Resume Writer's Association.[7]

Game Plan Recap

Monopoly is not really a game of chance; it's a game of strategy. It may seem like a fortunate roll of the dice is what's required to win when in fact it's careful strategy around which properties to acquire and which trades to make. Not relying on a single property to help you win is smart. Just like not relying on a single job search strategy will help you to accelerate your transition. Go ahead and use the job boards, but also pepper in some solid networking strategies, social media, personal outreach, connections with recruiters, and direct company information gathering. Once you have a more complete strategy, you're more likely to see the success you wanted, more readily.

In the last 49 days you have constructed a custom, effective job search system. You've identified key members of your network and wrangled up new members. You've filled in some skill gaps or put tangible plans in place to do so. And you've got your portfolio working for you and even mastered some of the essential conversations that you'll need to continue having throughout this journey. You are now officially better off than all the others in the rat race and that makes you smart. Reading this book was smart but implementing the principles means you're really smart. I'm rooting for you as you prepare to cross the finish line. Continue your strategic job search and don't lose focus on your goals. You've got the goods; I just know it.

PART III - EXPECTATIONS

Transitioning back into the workforce is not a walk in the park. There are days when you will struggle, feel disappointment, wonder if any of this is working, and so on. Yes, it's working but this is totally a wash, rinse, repeat methodology here. Most of these approaches are not one-time tasks. You will reach out to plenty of people on LinkedIn and some of them more than once. You will customize your resume frequently, you will attend several networking events, and participate in professional development regularly. I believe once you understand what's expected of you, you're more likely to do it.

Don't try to fool yourself; job searching on any scale is a little scary (new job, industry change), but sometimes a layoff can be that kick in the butt you needed to attain much-needed career satisfaction. Crying for a minute and feeling sad or angry are normal emotional responses during this time, but here are some thoughts that are intended to help you move forward, confidently.

CRUSH YOUR ROADBLOCKS
DAY 50

Layoffs happen to different people at different stages of life and sometimes our own, self-perceived challenges can keep us stalled. We are trapped behind the invisible wall like mimes. Sometimes mental barriers can be more powerful than reality so let me help you stomp out some of those emotional bullies with some effective solutions:

I'm too old - If you're not dead or dying, you're not too old. If you have come up against this, you may not be effectively conveying your value, modern tech skills, and willingness to do and continue doing the job. Jump on to some of the more modern social media trends like hosting an About.me page.

I'm a person of color - I am also a person of color, and I can almost guarantee my skin tone has never stopped me from reaching my goals. Once I've decided what I wanted, I found a way to achieve it. Complexion is not a viable excuse to give up or make assumptions about who's on the other end. You don't know their heritage or their story. This is insecurity as its core, and you must fight to overcome this hurt and self-imposed bias.

My accent is too strong - If this is true you can choose to work with a certified speech therapist. Otherwise, be sure to assemble some visual examples of your work. A picture is worth 1,000 words. You are great at what you do, in any language.

I'm overweight - I am not aware of this prohibiting any qualified person for a great opportunity. If you do feel strongly about your weight, there are far too many options out there for you (diet, exercise, accountability, even more aggressive surgical solutions). You can be in control of this area of your life. But the self-perceived bias against you may be totally in your own mind.

Application Tips:

- Ask yourself if it's worth holding onto those perceptions? Often times there is simply no merit in those beliefs.

- Address the elephant in the room with humor and dignity. "I know my _____(age, weight) may be a curiosity. I've learned that I am good at what I do and my _____ hasn't factored into my career; it's simply part of me."

- Sometimes the challenges are not just in your mind (like a criminal record); move on. Don't fret over another lost opportunity. Do your very best to stay optimistic and keep after the position and company that's right for you just the way you are.

RECOVERING FROM A LAYOFF

DAY 51

You've read of my volleying emotions and scant effort to try to get back into the workforce following my layoff. I must be totally transparent if you are to benefit from the mental recovery of a layoff. Even though downsizing is becoming more and more commonplace for struggling employers, it still takes an emotional toll on those of you affected.

If you're anything like me, the layoff wasn't the only disappointing thing that happened at that point in my life. My marriage was struggling, and my son was dealing with severe mental side effects from one of his prescribed medications. My relationship with God seemed to be suffering, and I was already feeling symptoms of depression. That season of my life caused me to think of the poem, Footprints, when Jesus said, "Where you see only one set of footprints in the sand, it was then that I carried you." I had to hold on to something, to avoid a complete nervous breakdown.

Now your situation may not be that dramatic, but yet, it could be worse. The bottom line for me was motivation and accountability. But you must know what strategies will keep you moving forward. A layoff can deliver a striking blow to your confidence, but it's your job not to let it pack your confidence in a suitcase and run away with it permanently. We all go through stuff when we lose the job that so much of our identity was tied to, but we have a responsibility to pick up the pieces and move on as best we can; as quickly as we can. My process of getting back on the horse realistically took a few years, but in hindsight I believe it would have been greatly shortened with the right inputs. So for today's application tips, allow me to give you a few shortcuts.

Application Tips:

- Watch what you're telling yourself just because you were laid off, doesn't mean you did an awful job. Most often, it was difficult but necessary to downsize.

- Overload yourself with positive words of affirmations and success stories. Document all of your major wins throughout your career. Seeing yourself in a more positive light will help you to continue motivating yourself back to 100 percent. Finding a scripture or quote to lean on can rebuild your confidence when you meditate on it regularly.

- Call an encouraging friend or a coach. Sometimes you can't see yourself the way others see you. You may need to let in some other viewpoints to stay stable.

- Stay productive. Don't allow yourself too much time to wallow. If you are continuing to get things done, your body will be so consumed with productivity that it has little time to reflect on any perceived failures.

- Face your fears head on. Practice your answers to tough interview questions and be ready to attack any doubts that creep up on you. You must be proactive!

- A layoff can be a real opportunity for you, too! If you're receiving a severance package and you find a new opportunity, you may get double for your trouble. Double income for a little while, and the added blessing of the needed time to discover your ideal career path.

ADDRESSING STICKY SITUATIONS
DAY 52

You Were Fired

This can be especially difficult, even embarrassing to address. Nonetheless, it is important that you do it right if this applies to you. Like most of these sticky situations, sticking to the facts will put you in the best possible light. If you were fired for falsifying timecards, state "I was separated from the company following a discrepancy with company records." If more information is requested, explain the situation: "I erroneously entered my working hours on my timecard, and my employment ended without opportunity to resolve the issue." They may dig deep, just avoid words and phrases such as fired, terminated, victim, or they didn't give me a chance.

Laid Off Multiple Times?

Rest assured. You are not alone in this boat. Our cyclical economy has left many professionals in a similar position. This one is a bit easier to defend. You simply state how excited you were to get back into using your _____, _____, and _____skills when the unthinkable happened. Another company that you were ready to commit service, and years to, began to sink financially and again, you were part of a strategic downsizing.

When I was laid off several years back, my prospective employers almost laughed it off since so many applicants had been part of a lay off. Don't stress about this. Just make sure you're staying productive between gigs and talk about those things.

Frequent Job Changes?

Some of us need more time to figure out what we want and in the process, we explore different career options. If this is you and you've held several different jobs in a short time frame—more than one change every two to four years—then you can simply focus on why you pursued each opportunity. Perhaps you really wanted to hone in on your project management skills so with great tenacity you went for it. Perhaps you just are best suited for temporary assignments because you get bored easily. (In this case, you can continue that track, because it is gaining popularity versus full-time, permanent employment). However, if you are ready to settle down then your job is to convince your new employer that you're in it for the long haul. Try the following scripts:

"My past positions have led me to a powerful conclusion: I have discovered a real strength in _____ and I'm looking for a home to share my expertise and gain new broader experience."

Or

"Yes, I've held a few positions in my recent past, but if you look carefully, you'll see a trend, as they were all in the _ _____ industry. I've been hungry to nurture my gifts in this area, and now I feel ready to contribute real, measurable results at a company of this magnitude."

Application Tips:

- In all of these situations, stick to the facts! Don't open mouth and insert foot by rambling on and on about all the possible reasons why you were a victim. Stick to what happened, what you learned from the situation, and how you plan to move forward and ensure it doesn't happen again! And for goodness' sake, never badmouth your former bosses or teams.

- Always look for ways to talk about your strengths, contributions, major results, and highly specialized skills. You always want the employers to want more of you!

DAILY MOTIVATION
DAY (53)

The following are motivational statements and quotes adopted from among the hundreds of confidence boosting tips I've posted on social media throughout the years. These may be great inspirational quotes you post on your mirror, wall, laptop, write them on your hand, do whatever is necessary to get these positive vibes infused into your thinking as you undergo this job transition.

- "It doesn't matter if your life has sucked up to this point. Faith is right now; the present is a present—a gift that you must proclaim today that your life is going to be great."
  — Pastor Sean R. Moore (Faith Christian Center, Phoenix, AZ)

- What is fear costing you? Fear of flying, costs you time in alternate travel! Fear of growing old causes you to miss what's happening right now! Fear of changing your career or company will cost you missed income, missed promotion, or missed opportunities for true career satisfaction!

- "Being fired is part of your career options."
  – Henrique de Castro (Former Yahoo COO)

- It's time to buckle down, reject those unproductive thoughts and seize the opportunities that are meant for you!

- As hard as it may be, resist the temptation to tell everyone you meet how difficult it has been for you for these last several months (or years) and instead focus on the value you bring, following up (not asking outright for a job), and being the first person to offer help! These strategies will keep people from avoiding your phone calls and deleting your emails. Your network might even forward your resume along to their hiring managers or HR department and vouch for you. After all, that's what you really wanted! YOUR TIME IS COMING!

- Motivate yourself! When you hear an inspirational message from a speaker or a book, it's still up to you to put those things into action. You can do it, once you set your mind on it!

- Embrace change; it usually brings about some pretty awesome stuff you would've never seen otherwise. New school, new job, career change, new house, new stocks, new career direction, promotion, going back to church. It's a little uncomfortable at first, then, before you know it, it fits like an old glove. #ChangeIsTheNewComfortable

- Stop putting so much focus on what you're not! Spend some time concentrating on what you are! You are skilled, experienced, qualified, loved and you know way more about your profession than most of us. So strut your stuff today. You got this!

- "You are not here merely to make a living. You are here in order to enable the world to live more amply, with greater vision, with a finer spirit of hope and achievement. You are here to enrich the world, and you impoverish yourself if you forget the errand."
  — Woodrow Wilson

- "The biggest mistake that you can make is to believe that you are working for somebody else. Job security is gone. The driving force of a career must come from the individual. Remember: Jobs are owned by the company; you own your career!"
  — Earl Nightingale

DAILY MOTIVATION (PART II)
DAY 54

- Dear Fear, You have told me lies and prevented me from doing the things I wanted to do and should have done. You are a miserable, wretched companion and one that I no longer am willing to be involved with. Signed, You!
  — Joyce Meyer

- We all have circumstances in our lives that can derail us and prevent us from reaching our goals if we pay excessive attention to them. Do what the crisis demands, but don't give it undue attention. Keep your conversation full of your goals, not your problems.
  — Joyce Meyer

- Fear comes in many forms (procrastination, doubt, dread) and it will make you do some crazy things (like browse Facebook when you know you should be making that phone call). What does fear look like for you?

- Your confidence does not come from your job. It stems from knowing your mission in this life and doing everything within your power to achieve it. As long as that can be said of you, no layoff or piece of negative feedback can keep you down.

- What does it take to discourage you? A rejection letter? Ten rejection letters? Zero phone calls this week? I remind you: "The tide goes out, but it always comes back in."
— Ricky Wilson

- Don't be that guy/gal who just asks everyone if they know of any opportunities. You must earn the right to ask. Network responsibly and people are more than happy to help. You help first!

DO FOR OTHERS DURING YOUR TRANSITION

DAY 55

When employers are interviewing the long-term unemployed (six months or longer), they want to know that you have been using your transition time wisely to get ready for your next opportunity. Here's one some simple thing you can do to make sure you have a great answer to that all-time favorite interview question: What have you been doing during your transition?

Volunteer! Make it regular and don't stop as soon as you get a job. Make sure your motives are pure, but pursue something that will allow you to keep your job skills fresh so your transition back to (or into) the workplace is seamless. People have mistakenly adopted the mindset that volunteering only equates to serving food in a soup kitchen, but there are so many areas that need volunteers why not explore some options that help you stay sharp in your profession.

Application Tips:

- If it's relevant, you can enter volunteer experience in your work experience section of your resume just like a paid position. That section is not bound by salary earned, it is the place to showcase your experience that helps position you for the job.

- If you don't include it in your experience section but create a separate "volunteer" heading, don't label it Community Service. This tag has become synonymous with parole status for criminal offenders. Use a headline, such as Community Involvement or Volunteer Service.

HELPING YOUR SPOUSE (OR PARTNER) UNDERSTAND THE SITUATION

DAY 56

Recently, I hosted an event called "Ain't Nothing Going On But the Rent"; inspired by the 1986 song, of the same title, by Gwen Guthrie. In her lyrics, she says, "You got to have a J-O-B if you want to be with me." In my work as a career manager, interview coach, job search strategist, I often hear of unsupportive spouses who are making the already challenging task of looking for meaningful work seem unbearable.

Nagging, constantly hearing "when are you going to find a job," and piling up your household chores because you're "not working anyway," can erode your confidence as a job seeker. At a time in your life when you need the most support from your loved one, you feel like you're under attack and constantly being devalued.

Put yourself in their shoes, your spouse may not have been in a job search in a long while so they are unfamiliar with the landscape of the job hunt in this century. They have no idea how fiercely competitive and technology-and-networking focused your search has to be. You are under a tremendous amount of pressure to provide for your family and the last thing you need is a reminder of what you're not doing.

Some of the things you can do to help them better support you, are:

- Have a heart-to-heart talk with them and be very transparent about your emotions.

- Talk to them about specific challenges you're facing (depression, lack of motivation, lack of financial support for some of the job search activities you need to do).

- Explain that just having a job is very different from having the right job that fits into your career plan.

- You be willing to cut out some of your lavish expenses (cell phone features, cable TV) to help reduce spending costs

- Ask them for grace and understanding that this process is expected to take at least two months for a professional at your level (may be quicker for certain blue collar and entry-level workers or longer for executive-level offices).

- Remind them that they can gently hold you accountable if you're not doing your part, so share your daily job search game plan (updating your resume, building a LinkedIn profile, navigating social media, networking, meeting with recruiters, informational interviewing, blogging, making phone calls) with them so they'll know what to watch out for and ask you about.

- If they are certified professional resume writers or bonafide HR professionals, they can offer feedback on your resume and career portfolio. Otherwise, explain that it would be more efficient to have a professionals' opinion.

Application Tips:

- Remember that they are dealing with emotions and concern, too.

- Ask for help throughout your search. Your significant other can help you with interview practice, prayer, and proofreading your portfolio documents.

DESPERATION IS NOT A PRETTY COLOR

DAY 57

You ever meet someone who was so hungry for something that they resorted to near-begging techniques to solicit help from their network, family, and even strangers? Yes, I said strangers! As we tackle the issue of fear, I want to send a clear reminder to job seekers and corporate ladder climbers that desperation is not a good look on anyone.

When a salesperson gets desperate their palms begin to sweat, they start settling for deals they wouldn't normally accept, and they begin to consider compromising their morals. Even Merriam-Webster defines desperation as a state of hopelessness leading to rashness. And while, some people will do some unthinkable things to try and stay afloat, and understandably so, it is very scary to think "if I don't get a job right now, I will be homeless," but be careful not to lose your place on the moral compass while you seek out your next opportunity. Here are some things you could do instead:

- Try temporary work (contract work), it will keep income coming in and keep your skills sharp!

- Innovate and start your own business.

- Meditate on this scripture (Galatians 6:9), Let us not

become weary in doing good, for at the proper time we will reap a harvest if we do not give up!

- Call your creditors, explain your situation (and what you're doing about it), then ask for an extension or forbearance on certain loans.

- Sit with a trusted financial advisor to make the best financial decisions during your transition.

If you've been behaving desperately, it's not too late to try a different more acceptable approach. As hard as it may be, resist the temptation to tell everyone you meet how difficult it has been for you for these last several months (or years) and instead focus on the value you bring, following up (not asking outright for a job), and being the first person to offer help! These strategies will keep people from avoiding your phone calls and deleting your emails. Your network might even forward your resume along to their hiring managers or HR department and vouch for you. After all, that's what you really wanted! Your time is coming.

I hope this poem encourages you:

RECHARGE

Lord, when my soul is weary and my heart is tired and sore,

and I have that failing feeling that I can't take it any more;

then let me know the freshening found in simple, childlike prayer,

when the kneeling soul knows surely that a listening Lord is there.

—Ruth Bell Graham

Application Tip:

If you have been guilty of this type of behavior, stop immediately and begin engaging your network from a place of value, not desperation.

Expectations Recap

Keeping the faith, avoiding desperation, and having a confidence that things will work out in your favor are paramount for you to survive this job transition season. I believe I lived through the depression, sadness, anger, and fear so you wouldn't have to. You don't have to learn from the school of hard knocks. It's OK to shred negative thoughts; they're not doing you any good anyway. It's OK to treat yourself to something special every once in a while. You're not strange because your job search has taken 3 or more months—that's just how long it takes. Your family can be supportive during this season if they understand how. Your network can support you if they know what you need. Humor is your friend, along with exercise and a good diet. All these ingredients blend together to make one heck of a job search recipe. So savor it and all the wondrous things you discover about yourself along the way. You can do it confidently!

PART IV - FIRST 90 DAYS

As I said earlier, it's not my intention to simply help you get hired. I want you to understand how to position yourself as a top employee within your first 90 days on the job. A job search is utterly incomplete without a plan to remain employed. Push through these final few sections so you can begin to understand how to manage your career versus simply working your job.

DON'T WAIT FOR A PINK SLIP: LIGHT A FIRE UNDER YOUR OWN BUTT

DAY 58

Did you know, according to the Bureau of Labor Statistics[8], that the average tenure for modern professionals is about 4.6 years in any given position? This means that an average employee will remain in a job for about 3 years before moving on. This is our ADD culture at play but it's also reflective of the cyclical nature of our American industries. There are no more guarantees. You just don't see people in a single job for 30 years then retiring with a nice gold watch. Think about it, in 2014-2015, we saw behemoths, Microsoft and Coca-Cola layoff over 18,000 workers each! Not to mention downsizes at Glaxo-Smith Kline, Macy's, and with educational budget slashes, we also saw thousands of teachers out of their already-underpaying jobs.

In fact, it's not all that uncommon for professionals to be laid off more than once throughout their career. So waiting for your tap on the shoulder instead of proactively managing your own career can prove to be a major mistake that can take years to recover from.

The costs of being unexpectedly laid off reach far beyond your bank account. If your confidence was already marginal, it could rub salt into your wound and simply crush your self-esteem. If your marriage is already strained, it could turn a merely uncomfortable situation into unbearable agony. Constant arguing over money is never fun. In fact, money spats are commonly considered the No. 2 cause of divorce in America.

Crossing your fingers and doing your best is an incomplete strategy. Paying attention to what's going on in your industry overall can give you an idea of what's to come. Looking at your company's financial reports will also keep you in the know. It should not come as a surprise that your firm is underperforming and layoffs might be on the horizon.

Application Tips:

- Update your resume every six to 12 months and keep it up to date.

- At least once per year, review Section 1 of this book and know your next career moves. Take a minute right now and set a future appointment on your calendar as a reminder.

- Stay connected with your network so it's not awkward to reach out and ask for help if you find yourself in need.

- Review your career plan from Day 3 and get yourself in position to acquire needed skills for your next step. A layoff doesn't have to equate to a setback in your career. You can use these transitions to continually move yourself forward. The key: You must have a plan in the first place.

- Create a Google alert to inform you of layoff announcements in your industry. This will prompt you to look deeper into your industry.

RESTORE YOUR CONFIDENCE

DAY 59

You may think that once you land a job the depression just magically goes away. That's not always the case. You've held on to your low self-confidence for so long that it became a part of you. Couple that with potentially degrading comments from your spouse or family, and it's no wonder you're still not curled up into a ball.

Your job was never the whole story anyway, so why would a replacement job, alone, be able to fill the void?

For me, it was unemployment coupled with marital woes. My husband was on the brink of walking out, my confidence had been dealt a near-fatal blow with the loss of my high-paying position as an engineer, and my faith in God had really be shaken and tested. For years I walked around actually saying that my confidence was gone, but it wasn't gone. It was simply waiting for me to rediscover it. To understand that my worth wasn't tied to a job, an employer, my paycheck, or my spouse, rather, it was rooted in God, and as it turns out, my roots were not as shallow as I once thought they were.

Application Tips:

Think about and even write down five to ten wonderful things about yourself. What makes you special? Meditate on each of these points as you go through your day. Let them encourage you and be a reminder of how much you have to offer the world.

If depression and low self-confidence do not plague you, then continue to remind yourself that you are more than your job and focus on the parts of you that you're proud of. This can help ward off depression.

Don't go looking for your dignity, it never left!

WHAT KIND OF EMPLOYEE ARE YOU?

DAY 60

There are diverse types of employees out there. This is not an exhaustive list, but should be used to identify which type most closely resembles you so you can understand why certain things may or may not be happening in your career.

1. Entitled - You can't understand why they haven't made you CEO by now. They should be grateful that you even decided to show up today, because your mere presence makes things happen. According to a 2014 survey I conducted, 100 percent of managers can't stand an entitled employee. Your fastest way up is to get low in humility.

2. Johnny Raincloud and Debbie Downer - Always shooting down other's ideas. You say things like "That'll never work, or we already tried it that way and it failed." Give others a chance to make their own mistakes and discoveries. Walking around like everything is doomed to failure doesn't project the optimism that's needed for groups to succeed in innovation. If you're absolutely sure the idea won't work, mention the aspects of the idea that might work! Find a morsel of positive in the sea of faults.

3. Victim - You got passed over for another promotion. "They" told you no to your third attempt at a salary increase. Your project failed, but it was because the expectations were too steep, and "they" only expected you to fail anyway! Your solution is to take ownership. If the expectations were unrealistic, then say so up front. If the salary increase conversation didn't go so well, ask them why and what, specifically, you need to do to secure it for next time. Then, show up and demonstrate that you've done it. You own your career. Stop waiting around for someone else to hand you things when you can go snatch them for yourself!

4. Chatterbox - You spend more time talking than you ever do working. You may have finished your work at lightening speed, but you're preventing your co-workers from completing theirs because you're constantly chatting with everyone. This is very disruptive and may start the cycle of avoidance. Don't be that guy (or gal), be respectful of others' time, and keep your comments very brief. Meet up after hours if you absolutely must converse.

5. Joker - Practical jokes were kind of, sort of funny in middle school, but now we're adults and you're still stuck in 7th grade. Being the office clown isn't usually the most desired title unless you're secretly preparing for a new career as a comedian. It's cool to lay out a little humor at a happy-hour gathering, but to constantly walk around performing slapstick comedy and telling knock-knock and a-priest-walked-into-a-bar jokes, can leave you on the wrong end of the punch

line.

6. Supervisor - Nothing is your job. Your only responsibility is to make sure others are doing what they should be doing. You never choose to get your hands dirty. Perhaps you figured, you've paid your dues, so you've chosen a career of directing everyone else's actions. The problem with this is that your skills will become rusty and you will lower your own marketability. No one wants to hire a leader who couldn't get the work done themselves. Get in the game!

Application Tip:

Honestly assess which type of employee you have been and write down your action plan to incorporate some of the solutions provided once you land in your next role

I seem to have the most in common with _____

_____

_____

_____

To impact my perception in the workplace, I will _____

_____

_____

_____

BONUS :
MORE ON PERSONAL
BRANDING AND
ESTABLISHING YOUR BRAND

Your brand is the skill or trait that you want to be best known for. Think, what do I want to specialize in? In what area do you wish to be the go-to expert? Now, you have to start developing those specialty muscles. If you want to be the recognized subject matter expert in enterprise-wide change projects, you need to campaign for a smaller, visible project so you can prove that you are shrewd enough to tackle a more bottom-line-impacting assignment.

In every task there is something you can learn. Establish what you will and can gain from each project and understand that your measure of success (in addition to monitored metrics) can be fulfillment of your skill-building objectives. For example, if you are looking to move into management, but you and your mentor have determined that you need more experience with strategy development request to be on the planning team for a new program or to sit in on the project acceptance committee. This will expose you to all sorts of strategic decision making in real time.

One of my clients who already supervises a team of 20 people was looking to move into a more senior leadership position but lacked experience at that level so she requested to start sitting in on interviews for candidates pursuing opportunities at her current level. She was initially met with resistance but after a necessary sit down with her boss, she was granted access to this new level of decision making.

The moral is whatever you're looking to get from your career can be obtained if you understand what you need, are willing to ask for it, and can demonstrate your ability to perform at that next level.

Conclusion

There is no magic formula to job searching, but if I were a betting person, I would wager on the job seeker who was employing multiple job search methods, had a clear goal, and was willing to follow the game plan laid out in this book.

Being handed your pink slip can be a hard pill to swallow, but even more difficult when you feel lost and confused about how to get back to work. So much has changed in the marketplace. Human resource departments are now mostly automated, and you are now armed and dangerous to navigate the tricky terrain of the job search. From establishing goals to understanding ATS, building effective portfolios, using social media like a savvy job seeker, networking, interviewing like a champ, accepting your ideal offer, staying encouraged, and establishing your brand as a top performer, you have solved the puzzle of how to get back to work in 60 days. It's still OK if you're not employed by the end of this book, just keep doing what you're doing and reference back as often as necessary until you have that offer letter in your hand.

When you receive your walking papers you can either stay curled up in the corner or you can crush that stupid pink slip, put on your big kid pants, and get to work. The choice is yours.

NOTES

1. Napoleon Hill, Think and Grow Rich (New York: The Random House Publishing Group, 1937), 38.

2. John C. Maxwell, How Successful People Think (New York: Hachette Book Group, 2009), 8.

3. Valorie Burton, Successful Women Think Differently: 9 Habits to Make You Happier, Healthier, & More Resilient (Eugene: Harvest House Publishers, 2012), 148.

4. Financial Peace University™, http://www.daveramsey. com/store/financial-peace-university/financial_peace_ university_lifetime_membership/prod614.html, September 16, 2015.

5. Carla A. Harris, Expect to Win: 10 Proven Strategies for Thriving in the Workplace (New York: Plume, 2009), 95.

6. Statistic Brain, http://www.statisticbrain.com/reading-statistics/, July 14, 2014.

7. The National Resume Writers' Association, http://www. thenrwa.com.

8. Bureau of Labor Statistics, "Employee Tenure Summary," http://www.bls.gov/news.release/tenure. nr0.htm, September 18, 2014.

* Names indentified with this mark have been fictionalized. They do represent actual people but due to the sensitive nature of job searching, they have chosen to share their story but remain anonymous.

Made in the USA
San Bernardino, CA
08 January 2016